P9-CKK-379

Never Marry a Girl with a Dead Father

RENEWALS 458-4574
DATE DUE

WITHDRAWN
UTSA Libraries

Never Marry a Girl with a Dead Father

Women's Troubled Relationships in Realist Novels

Helen Hayward

I.B.Tauris *Publishers*
LONDON • NEW YORK

Published in 1999 by I.B.Tauris & Co Ltd
Victoria House, Bloomsbury Square, London WC1B 4DZ
175 Fifth Avenue, New York, NY 10010
Website: http://www.ibtauris.com

In the United States and Canada distributed by St. Martin's Press
175 Fifth Avenue, New York, NY 10010

Copyright © Helen Hayward, 1999

The right of Helen Hayward to be identified as the author of this work has
been asserted by the author in accordance with the Copyright, Designs and
Patents Act, 1988.

All rights reserved. Except for brief quotations in a review, this book, or any
part thereof, may not be reproduced, stored or introduced into a retrieval
system, or transmitted, in any form or by any means, electronic,
mechanical, photocopying, recording or otherwise, without the prior written
permission of the publisher.

ISBN 1 86064 186 5 (hardback)
    1 86064 187 3 (paperback)

A full CIP record for this book is available from the British Library
A full CIP record for this book is available from the Library of Congress

Library of Congress catalog card: available

Typeset in Bookman 10 on 12½ pt by The Midlands Book Typesetting
Company, Loughborough
Printed and bound in Great Britain by WBC Ltd, Bridgend

Contents

Acknowledgements

I am indebted to four people who made this book possible: my original supervisor Professor Malcolm Bowie who remained intelligent throughout and knew when to push; my friend Anita Phillips who provided first-hand encouragement and bracing criticism; my editor Philippa Brewster who challenged me to convert an effortful PhD thesis into a readable book; and my husband John Armstrong whose critical eye I was at first unable to use, but with time came to appreciate.

1

Introduction

This book carries a warning – never marry a girl with a dead father – counsel I overheard more than once in adolescence, around the time of my own father's final heart attack. The warning is meant literally: it is best to avoid having a relationship with a woman whose father died when she was young. Not because of his death, but because of the problematic life he continues to have in her imagination.

Death catastrophically ends whatever illusions a girl may have of her father as all-powerful. She sees him vulnerable and broken. Yet at the same time, the untimely timing of death makes adult acquaintance impossible; she carries a child's image of him into later life, unrelieved by the shadings and crosshatchings which longer experience brings.

Although a model in a picture can't say anything, her look can tell us much. Edgar Degas painted the daughter of his friend Monsieur Rouart on a number of occasions. At the age of ten on the knee of her industrialist father, as a young woman alongside her mother, and slightly later, by her father's side once more. A final painting shows Hélène as a young woman standing alone in her father's study. She looks out from behind an outsized mahogany chair, empty and turned to the viewer; to the left three Egyptian statues, also enlarged, sit in a metal and glass case; behind her hangs a landscape and a Corot sketch of a peasant crouching; along the top right is an ornate Eastern wallpaper in red and gold. Her expression is abstract and melancholy, her dress is blue and conventionally cut, and her hair picks out the burnished gold of the frame and wall-paper. Neither father nor mother are present, yet her father's chair takes up a quarter of the painted surface. The antique statues face away from the desk, inside a cabinet next to a pile of papers. The daughter's look is oblique, her expression ambiguous, leaving the viewer free to speculate. In this painting Hélène Rouart compels interpretation; without it she, and particularly her gaze, remains opaque. It is as if in the absence of a viewer Hélène wouldn't fully exist; sphinx-like she demands that the viewer should work to make sense of her.

Hélène Rouart's absent father haunts the picture. Is this girl, a viewer might ask, the subject of this painting, or simply the largest object in Monsieur Rouart's collection? And her askance look, does it express an allegiance to her parents, or her distance from them? More deeply, does her look imply an opposition to her father or a liaison with him? Is Hélène daughter first and woman second, or the other way round? That is, is she mature? This last question is central. Where do Hélène's loyalties ultimately lie, with her parents or with herself?

In fact Hélène Rouart's father was still very much alive when this picture was painted, but I have come to see the girl with the literally dead father as a metaphor for the condition of many women; in a metaphorical sense, many women have a dead father. Isn't the young girl's fantasy of a father as all-powerful always shattered in adolescence; isn't her internal image of him always, in some sense, still a child's?

This is a picture of a woman who isn't mature because imaginatively she still exists as an item in someone else's imagination – her father's. The Hélène Rouart girl, the girl with a dead father, symbolises the kind of woman who seems to live at a slight remove from her own life, who suffers silently, who gives only quiet signs of distress. I am interested in women to try to live through others, through lovers, friends, husbands, children - anyone other than through and for themselves. Do they see in others a vitality inaccessible in themselves? At a certain moment, why do they start defending against excitement, fearing rather than pursuing it? Why do they organise their lives so as to play down what interests them, for the sake of something else; why do they feel compelled to keep the kitchen spotless while neglecting the cultivation of their powers? What stops these women taking up the thread of their own lives more vigorously, imaginatively, and enjoyably?

I take the girl with the dead father as the emblem of this female persona; her literal condition as a metaphor of the type of psychological condition – or state of the soul – which can mask and mar a woman's life. But not only as an emblem. The girl with the dead father, I believe and argue in this book, illuminates in an especially vivid way one of the roots of this existential paralysis. A girl whose father has died in her imagination – who is dead to her symbolically – may also find it hard to perceive whoever comes after him as potent. However a girl whose father has died in reality, *after* he has already died to her imaginatively, is likely to find it hardest of all. Why? Because she fails to bring her father into line with other men, so that he remains imaginatively bigger, better, and bolder than them – just as when he first took her on his knee as a child.

These are the questions that interest me, but where to turn for answers? Feminism has pointed an acute finger at external, social structures – the complex of work practices, prejudices, educational patterns, and family arrangements which go under the general name of patriarchy. It would be naïve to doubt the real impact of these structures on  women's lives but the women I am thinking of, myself not least, live in a post-feminist society – one which has largely accepted the feminist case and which in most areas presents women with just as many, or as few, encouragements and obstacles as it does to men. It is the inner constraints, not the outer ones, to which my attention is directed. And the girl with the (literal or metaphorical) dead father comes in here because she isn't suffering an external impediment. It is, precisely, something which is going on inside her that makes her sidestep life.

And in any case I want to draw a different point, which is that one's outer life and internal life are rarely continuous with each other. They may overlap in places but they are just as likely to clash in others. This leads to a larger point, which is that while women have been liberated from a large number of external constraints, women as individuals are still subject to inner constraints which no amount of equal opportunities and legislation can loosen. If inner freedom can be achieved it will come harder and slower than civil rights.

Inner struggles are timeless; if they can be exacerbated by social conditions, they cannot be fully explained by them. In the eyes of the world a woman may appear promising and may actually be well-situated, while in her own eyes she is just a pushy adolescent. Inner constraints, invisible to the eye, are hard to detect, and harder still to lift; a woman's actual shyness – and whatever it is she is shielding in her shyness – can't be easily grasped. We see something similar in the manner such a woman relates to a significant other. This is because a woman, to the extent she experiences herself as feminine, tends to overinvest in a significant other. Most girls, and many women, imaginatively project special – and ultimately parental – qualities on to the person closest to them. The degree to which they perceive qualities like autonomy and insight in this other is a reflection of how keenly they feel their lack in themselves.

The major discourse of inner constraint is of course that initiated by Freud. Freud's elaborations of the idea of hysteria, in particular, have shaped the ways we think about the internal lives of women. The notion of hysteria, in partic-ular – the female malady par excellence – has its ancient origin in the too graphic image of the 'wandering womb', the sexually starved organ supposedly attacking various parts of the afflicted woman causing convulsions, screaming fits, paralysis – the kind of behaviour called hysterical ever since and to which women have often been thought essentially prone. The medical analysis of such fits became the preoc-cupation of the eminent Parisian doctor Jean Charcot towards the end of the 1880s. At the famous Salpêtrière hospital he catalogued and classified the various stages and sequences of the dramatic performances which his many female patients conveniently provided.

The young Sigmund Freud was among the large number of students who attended Charcot's fashionable public demonstrations. The crucial step which Freud took and which Charcot never did was to pursue not a description of hysterical performances but an explanation of what might be going wrong inside. To pursue, in other words, a psychological model of a suffering person which would give some insight into the genesis of such wretched exhibitions. Up to this point the leading thesis was that hysterical fits were the result of specific organic disorders or lesions of the brain. These were thought to explain the array of symptoms: loss of motor control, amnesia, screaming, anaesthesia (Charcot's case studies included a woman who apparently felt no distress when her forearm was skewered by a hat pin) and so on.

The superiority of a psychological rather than organic explanation became apparent when it was shown that hysterical symptoms frequently failed to tally with physical conditions. The location of a paralysis, for example, would not cohere with the organic structure of the limb in question. More positively, increasing attention to the prehysterical condition of patients suggested that there might be psychological factors contributing to the onset of the illness.

The return to a psychological explanation has a very important further consequence. What seemed of interest now were not the flamboyant symptoms, the grimaces, leaps etc., but the surrounding constellation of personal history and inner life. In this way Freud was able to present an account of hysteria in which dramatic cases were seen as continuous with, indeed essentially the same as, a number of less dramatic instances. A psychological model of flamboyant hysteria came to be seen as applicable equally to women who were, as we significantly say, quietly hysterical.

Freud's most famous case study – of a young woman he called Dora – sought to trace the origins of hysteria in repressed sexuality. Freud argued that what Dora suffered from was a displacement of unacceptable and disturbing sexual excitement into somatic symptoms.

In his study of Dora, Freud interprets this young woman's rage as an attack on a sexual double standard that passed her, in silent exchange, from her father to the husband of her father's lover. This is however only half the story; the rest concerns what went on in Dora's imagination during this intricate exchange. While Dora is clearly a pawn in her father's game, she is also fascinated by the other man's interest in her, which is why she feels conflictual *and* excited. It is this half of a woman's story, made up of impulses, images, thoughts, and ideas (as opposed to symptoms, behaviour, and social conditions), which promises to shed most light on a form of suffering which remains a feature of modern life.

Dora is infuriated by Freud's interpretations – that she is turned on by the man who makes passes at her, and that the purse she fondles during her sessions represents her sexual organs, and especially by Freud's eagerness to speculate on her motives. And yet her growing distrust of Freud hints at something more profound, which is her distrust of herself. The more fervently she resists Freud's interventions and tests his patience, the more she comes to depend on him – and fly from herself. Dora can't bear the vulnerability he makes her feel, which is why she makes sure their time together is cut short. Having first approached Freud with the hope of recovery, she later delights in her treatment going badly. As if, having reached a certain level of intimacy, she feels she must end it.

Dora's stubbornness made her famous in psychoanalytic circles; another woman with similar problems, less famous but well known to novel readers, is the oddly modern Sue Bridehead in Thomas Hardy's *Jude the Obscure*. After appealing to Jude for understanding, and succeeding, Sue starts to resent his sympathy for her, no longer wanting it. She is led to say one thing while feeling quite another, which is perhaps why she comes across as a prudish free-lover. Several times she leaves Jude, only to return, guilty at his unhappiness. Sue's bitterness for English society is grounded, in that the townspeople really do hold her free-living against her; and yet, ultimately, it is her own self-criticism that damages her, and drives her husband to distraction. For many readers Thomas Hardy presents a dark view of human relations. Female sexuality is for him always troubled: in *Jude the Obscure* it is not by chance that Sue Bridehead upsets an otherwise romantic narrative by her single- and bloody-mindedness.

Of course Freud's thoughts about hysteria were only just beginning. In a much later paper, 'Those Wrecked by

Success', Freud takes up again the theme of female hysteria. Significantly in this later work it is to a literary case, rather than one of his own patients, that Freud's attention is devoted.

I too follow the lead of heroines in classic novels, tracing through the problems in their inner lives, and generalising from these. This is similar to Freud's approach in *Studies on Hysteria*, which he himself believed were a series of sophisticated stories. In a period of strong scientific materialism, Freud was initially keen to keep on the side of science and pathology: the prevalence in hysteria of symptoms ranging from anaesthesia, paralysis, cough, stutter, vaginism, and vomiting meant that an organic explanation couldn't be ruled out. Only when he hit what he called the bedrock of femininity did he extend his research to sexual and cultural spheres. Convinced that the solution to hysteria lay less with bodily lesions than with voluptuous satisfaction, and its repression and denial, it made sense to turn to literature at this point.

In 'Those Wrecked by Success', Freud singles out Rebecca West in Ibsen's *Rosmersholm* to dramatise what happens when a woman steals another woman's husband. Freud focuses on Rebecca's motives, not her symptoms, emphasising the imaginative rather than physical effects of her wishes. Haunted by her theft, Rebecca refuses her employer Rosmer's advances, fearing what may happen if she conceives a child with him – as she secretly wishes. But then, on discovering Rosmer is her father, Rebecca turns on herself and jumps off a bridge – just as earlier she'd encouraged Rosmer's wife to do. Freud talks about Rebecca as if she were a real woman caught between two realities, one real and the other imaginative. In desiring what isn't hers for the having – another woman's lover – Freud suggests that she is punished by hysteria. Interestingly, while Freud is often criticised for overlooking the mother's role in the hysterical scenario, in this analysis the mother is central – Rebecca's desire for Rosmer (the father) being interpreted as a suppressed desire for his wife (the mother).

In Freud's hands, *Rosmersholm* becomes a fable about hysteria. A woman who shrugs away her mother and turns to her father will then experience her femininity in a passive

– and potentially destructive – way, thus inviting a hysterical response. By encouraging Rosmer's wife to jump to her death, and thus refusing to identify with her as a woman, Rebecca loses all sense of why she feels and acts as she does – as if suddenly possessed by the feminine knowledge she has repressed. As if, in her confusion, she is pushed to enact the knowledge she can't absorb. The meaning of this fable is that Rebecca's longing for her father forbids her to possess him; moreover she is mistaken in treating her haven with Rosmer as her rightful home. Taking his analysis of the play one step further, Freud suggests that a girl's love for her father – unlike a boy's for his mother – rarely dissolves in the ordinary course of things. Rather it keeps her in a state of erotic suspense from which she seeks release in marriage and childbirth. Obviously this attitude is questionable today: women no longer feel impelled to marry and give birth. However women continue to fantasise and to inhabit imaginative worlds which inevitably contain sexual attraction and fertility; so that even if they choose an unorthodox path, they still have to find ways of satisfying their eroticism.

What is striking about Rebecca's story is the apparent absence of her mother from it; although her mother drifts in and out of her imagination, she is absent as an emotional mainstay. This is because when a girl has desires she considers unseemly, her impulse is to imagine that her mother, rather than herself, disapproves of them. Hence her apparent withdrawal from her mother. However because at a deep level such a girl has an investment in the disapproval she lodges in her mother, their lasting separation isn't an option. This bond between mother and daughter often goes unnoticed, particularly as, from the girl's point of view, she feels closest to her father. This closeness is vital, since it protects the girl from her mother's – supposed – disapproval. A daughter's love for her father is often special, finding expression as reverence and affection; many girls need their father's favour if they are to escape what they experience as their mother's ban on erotic pleasure. But this is futile, since a girl's idealisation of her father has as its reverse a preoccupation with her mother from which there is no escape – even from a father worth revering. This is why many grown-up daughters appear openly affectionate toward their fathers but decidedly awkward with their mothers.

Hysteria is a good focus for thinking about the kind of women who interest me, because hysteria essentially involves giving up on living and thinking for oneself, and instead gives over one's identity to another who is experienced as more powerful. It was Freud's primary positive contribution to locate the ground of hysteria in identification – that is, in the attempt to live (for whatever reasons) through another. Hence hysteria is often implicated in love, in those relationships in which one person thinks they cannot live without another and in which they look to the other as a surrogate source of authority, finding none in themselves. And hence also we can see maturity as the converse of hysteria – for maturity is partly constituted by a capacity not to identify; the capacity to hold on to a separate and distinct (and more modest) sense of oneself; and with this the correlative possibilities of living for and through oneself; ultimately of being able to take oneself seriously.

On the negative side, Freud's analysis of the case of Dora onwards is burdened with difficulties. There is reason to doubt the adequacy of his almost exclusive concern with sexuality as the formative factor in hysteria. Sexuality is only one instance of our potential to make good, exciting, and intimate things happen; it is just one aspect of the larger issue of forming a relationship. What I have taken from Freud are his two big suggestions that hysteria is internal and psychological, and that it occurs in quiet as well as flamboyant forms.

What happens in a woman's life for her to start defending against the kind of excitement which, up to that point, kept her girlish self alive? Specifically, what leads a woman to put her need for control over and above her desire for excitement? Why, I wonder, are women who feel under pressure within inclined to defend against the things they are strongly drawn to, even when these may be valuable? It is impossible, I think, to answer these questions without considering a woman's thoughts and feelings for the people she is closest to, and especially the person she directs her strongest emotional appeal to. A woman doesn't reach a hysterical impasse all by herself; for a full understanding one has to look at her relations to her partner, parents, and friends, for they too – to the extent hysterical elements are alive in them – are implicated in her dilemma. This is why hysteria is best explained in terms of what I call hysterical relations, a silent pact arising out of unstable elements between – at least – two people. Such pacts are always shared; hysteria would be short-lived were it not fanned by this kind of intimacy.

This sets my ideas apart from the Freudian view that hysteria is all about an individual's desire – as opposed to the vulnerability brought to the surface by close intimacy. In Freud's theory it is always sexual desire that lies behind hysterical conflict. This, it would now appear, is simplistic: women who experience inner conflict are often wary of extreme pleasures, of which sexuality is an important kind. But they are also wary of the excitement surrounding intel-lectual, creative, and aggressive wishes. Freud, it seems, put sexual matters before existential ones. Since attitudes to sexuality have been relaxed it seems clear that what presses on women are larger questions relating to their existence – to their reasons for being in the world at all – rather than their sexual preferences. They may derive intense pleasure from sexual activity, but few women assume that this, on its own, gives meaning to their lives.

Instead of applying Freud I have turned to the pre-Freudian literature which seeks to investigate the inner lives of women, but which does not treat sexuality as more than one of a number of relevant factors. Indicative of this more generous focus is the way in which such literature traces the longer path through a process of a woman's more or less successful maturing. This is, incidentally, contrastive to the case study approach of much psychoanalytic literature. While in such cases we may learn a great deal about a patient, up to and especially during treatment, we rarely get to hear much about what happens afterwards; the narrative of development is broken not when it reaches a natural conclusion but when the analysts' sessions end. Add to this the fact that in the case studies our grasp of those to whom a woman relates is always uncomfortably filtered through what she says about them in her sessions. The analyst, unlike the novelist, cannot take us into the point of view of other characters in her life.

To look for these qualities of narrative continuity and multiple points of view is, of course, to appeal to the tradition of the realist novel in, above all, its classic phase from the mid-nineteenth to early twentieth century.

Unlike various post-modern critics, I don't have a problem with traditional novels for being traditional. I like George Eliot for being all-knowing, and for telling us exactly what Adam Bede and Dorothea Brooke are like. On the other hand I find some of Freud's descriptions of Dora off-putting; for example, when Dora is overcome by disgust, Freud describes this as 'the unpleasurable feeling which is proper to the tract of mucous membrane at the entrance to the alimentary canal'. If someone is naturally defensive, as Dora clearly was and I certainly am, the last thing you want is for someone to boast of their insights into you. Somehow novels get around this stickiness: while I may identify with Anna Karenina while reading Tolstoy's novel, I am also aware of *not* being her, and this encourages an acceptance of the narrator's views on her – in a way that would be impossible were they directed at me personally. Moreover, however acute Tolstoy's insights into Anna are, the surrounding fictional world is always there to make sense of it, and to shed a softening light.

The fact that many women see aspects of themselves in the heroines they read about is, I think, a good thing. Novelists have a way of making the troubling aspects of their heroines *interesting*; a character trait which in a friend or oneself is awkward or tiresome can, treated by Balzac, become absorbing – even fascinating. The kind of learning that goes on in a chair with a book can never be tested, and will never hold its own against formal tests, nonetheless it has the potential to make learning about oneself – through, for example, the stories of Eugenie Grandet, Anna Karenina, or Isabel Archer – a pleasure, rather than a self-conscious, circular, and at times painful activity. This kind of learning may look passive, and admittedly there are those who learn little from novels, but the potential for increasing one's awareness through reading is always there.

Hysteria, in Freud's view, results from a girl's overreaction to early erotic excitement. Initially he thought that sexuality often enters girls' lives too soon, before the organisational part of themselves – the ego – had developed enough to deal with it. Hence when excitement enters a girl's awareness suddenly, she treats it as dangerous and quickly gets rid of it. No memory is kept, so that when memories later emerge they reflect the act of *remembering* the experience, often coloured by embarrassment or humiliation, rather than the actual experience. Freud's key insight was that hysteria can always be traced back to the wish to attract the interest of an important other. Every form of hysteria, which includes symptoms, actions, behaviour, fantasies, and memories, are 'aimed at another person – but mostly at the prehistoric, unforgettable other person who is never equalled by anyone later'.[1] This person, never equalled nor forgotten, appears with the first signs of a girl's awareness, and is hence formed by feelings and memories which arise after the originating events. Although the gender of this important other is unclear, his (or her) origin in an early relationship suggests an idealised parent figure.

When it comes to thinking about early loved ones often it is our reminiscences, more than our memories, that spring to mind. A catch-phrase of Freudian theory is that hysterics suffer from reminiscences – a claim in itself poetic and vague. In my understanding a reminiscence is an overloaded memory, on to which feelings from another memory – now repressed – have been transferred. Whereas a memory *recalls* a past event, a reminiscence *relives* it. Because a reminiscence contains fantasies which have escaped the ego's notice – unlike a memory which the ego is able to repress – it can remain in consciousness. If however these feelings do emerge, and the fantasy is unveiled, the feelings are likely to be spontaneously repressed.

The unhappiness which is fuelled by reminiscences is what Freud and others aimed to lighten. This aim distinguished them, once and for all, from doctors who sought to relieve physical pain. Recovery of a sense of well-being – the French use the phrase 'bien dans sa peau', meaning to feel good in one's skin – is not the same as recovering health or dissolving symptoms. A woman who seeks relief from unhappiness need not be ill, except in the existential sense. She is not looking for someone to make her well physically, but for someone to help her reach a positive understanding of her inner world. She is looking for someone who will encourage her to respond to symbolic aspects of reality, through her imagination and perception enlivening it. A woman who has lost her sense of well-being is out of touch with herself, the creative part that makes everything meaningful.

Another difference between my approach to women's psychological difficulties and that of Freud, is that rather than looking at unusual, extreme, or abnormal cases, and using these to shed light on normal women, I consider the hysterical potential of normal women, often with no medical history. Many people are intrigued by the Pappenheim sisters who murdered their mother with an axe; but for me the proper focus for understanding what troubles women in their experience of femininity lies not in spectacular anomalies, but in their ordinary lives, which, although unremarkable, can be hugely nuanced – especially when presented by Tolstoy or George Eliot. Having said this, each of the heroines I discuss share something significant with Freud's hysterical patients. While their thoughts don't become dissociated and their limbs don't go into spasm, at a certain moment, instead of responding creatively to life's excitements, they start reacting against them.

This defensiveness does not however weaken them. It would be false to suggest that Isabel Archer and Anna Karenina are weak characters; for all their suffering, they are resilient, as if strengthened by the feelings of longing and resistance that dominate their emotional lives. What I mean by longing is the desire to unite with a loved one; resistance, in contrast, is the impulse to keep a loved one away; together, these forces channel and regulate the wishful and defensive strivings in each of us. When a woman becomes hysterical this regulatory function fails, so that she swings from wanting to embrace a loved one to wanting to reject him (or her) altogether. In opposition to Freud, who saw hysteria as an effect of the repression of wishful impulses, I suggest that the key lies in resistance – in the act of holding out *against* excitement, for fear of giving in to longing for it.

The kinds of relationships which I call hysterical are more likely to occur when there has been a strong bond between daughter and father. Gwendolen Harleth and Isabel Archer are without living fathers, but this doesn't stop their close relationships being coloured by the fathers they miss. In the imaginative life of many girls the father is erotically and symbolically charged, sometimes to the point of representing everything that is attractive and significant to her. Before a daughter can end her relationship to such a father she has to discover what has gone into it, which includes those parts of herself that she has invested in him. The girl with a dead father lacks this understanding, which is why in every later relationship she assumes – unknowingly – the role of daughter. This makes her a disconcerting lover, since while outwardly she seeks a lover, she remains imaginatively engaged with her father – hence making the couple a three-some. A girl's inability to be fully intimate may not initially show; only with time will her failure to appreciate her lover – chosen for his (or her) resemblance to her dead father – emerge. It may take years for it to dawn that instead of relating to her lover as a lover, reciprocally, she is relating to him as a daughter, unreciprocally.

I realise that when talking about Isabel Archer I refer to her as if a real person, rather than a character in a novel. In my mind Isabel is *as if* real; while reading Henry James' novel, and later in memory, Isabel Archer is imaginatively alive. This experience can, I suggest, be more intense with a character in a novel than with the people one knows in real life; often it is possible to get closer to a hero or heroine, with the help of an insightful narrator, than with friends and acquaintances who protect themselves from intimacy at crucial moments. Successful realist novels don't simply describe a character in depth, they bring them to life from within and without, giving a rounded picture. Twentieth-century novels also have this capacity, but to a lesser degree, simply because they tend to follow the thoughts and feelings – the consciousness – of one character. This can be utterly convincing, but beguiling too, because the reader is dominated by the point of view of this character. In, say, Virginia Woolf's later novels, the reader knows no more nor less than what the central consciousness knows; whatever she or he withholds from the reader remains unknown: one could speculate for days why Clarissa Dalloway sleeps in a single bed, or whether Lily Briscoe secretly fancies Mr

Ramsey, but it would be in vain. Modernist writers assume it is more life-like to leave certain things unsaid, and to keep the natural reserve of a character intact: these writers have a point, however in view of what troubles women generally it seems more helpful when a novel explores inner complexities than chooses to avoid them.

Notes

1. *Complete Letters of Sigmund Freud to Wilhelm Fliess 1887–1904*, Edited by Jeffrey Moussaieff Masson (Harvard, 1985), p. 213

2

The Hysterical Daughter: Balzac's *Eugenie Grandet*

From a psychoanalytic point of view, the short nineteenth century may be said to have run from 1830 to 1895, that is from the early novels of Balzac to Freud's *Interpretation of Dreams*. Balzac is the first author – the first who has continued to hold a major position in world literature – to present a systematic and intimate psychological investigation of human relations. Nothing happens by chance in Balzac's 'Human Comedy', from which *Eugenie Grandet* is an early work; our lives only seem improbable, says the narrator, when we 'omit to cast, as it were, a psychological light on our impulsive decisions by failing to reveal the hidden causes that make them inevitable. Many people prefer to reject the conclusions, rather than to measure the strength of the links, the bonds, and the connections which form the hidden psychological chains that lead from one event to another'[1]. Within Balzac's world other people are not enigmatic; they only seem so when the links between their thoughts and actions are overlooked. By focusing on these hidden chains Balzac describes Eugenie Grandet's life as a series of meaningful moments, rather than a shadowy dance of fate: first describing her as a girl, suddenly aware of her sexual nature, then as a woman, alive to her wish for love beyond her family, and finally as an older woman who, despairing of love, sits out the years remaining to her.

Eugenie Grandet's story is a radically simple one. Precious little happens at the level of action, apart from the meeting between Eugenie and her cousin, at which point the novel opens. Eugenie is the only daughter of well-off provincial parents; of a father who aspires to ever greater wealth and power and a mother who lets providence decide her fate – and consequently dies young. Charles Grandet arrives at his uncle's house in Saumur, a small provincial town, in the middle of Eugenie's birthday celebrations. While Grandet, a rich miser, welcomes his nephew, his daughter Eugenie sits back, quietly agog at her cousin's finery. When the next morning Charles discovers his father has committed suicide – a bankrupt – Eugenie's feelings blossom into love. In contrast, on hearing of his brother's death Grandet urges his nephew Charles not to grieve, but to aspire to quick profits overseas. But not before Eugenie and Charles fall in love, meteorically for Eugenie and gratefully, compensatorily, for Charles.

Eugenie persuades her cousin to accept her gold coins, entrusted to her by her father, and shortly after Charles departs to seek his fortune. Grandet, on discovering his daughter's gift, flies into a rage; Eugenie stands up to him, but later allows him to lock her in her room. At this point Madame Grandet, a key but shadowy figure, takes to her bed and soon dies. Two years pass, and again Grandet confronts Eugenie over her gift to Charles – whom, during his travels, has lost touch with Eugenie. Then another two years, with Grandet, helpless and vexed, now on his death-bed. Seven years – and one letter – after leaving Eugenie, Charles returns: not to her, but to Paris and a profitable society marriage. Incapable of spite, Eugenie makes Charles's marriage possible by paying off his creditors, and determines to make a fruitless marriage to de Bonfons. After he dies, she lives on very simply in Saumur, cared for by

Nanon, the family's loyal servant, and devoting herself to charity. The novel ends as it begins, in darkness, with the narrator looking through the living room window at Eugenie, now sallow, noble, and lonely. It is a horror story of sorts, a quiet and relentless tale of a woman's decline.

As a novel *Eugenie Grandet* is deceptively plain and peculiarly distressing. Balzac is at pains to show the inevitability of his heroine's fate, and the obliviousness of the people around her to it. At its simplest, it is the story of a heroine who, uncomfortable with what her parents have given her, tries to give it away. But this attempt to distance herself from her inheritance fails, since her parents' provision turns out to be essential to her. Quite apart from material privilege, Eugenie never takes possession of crucial aspects of herself; treating her parents, lover, and inheritance as objects to keep to herself and to handle as keepsakes – kept for the sake of keeping – rather than possessions whose value is reflected in their use. Feeling she doesn't deserve what she has been given, and fearful that it increases her value beyond her private estimation, she gives what is most valuable about her away, and so becomes an heiress of nothing.

Despite the esteem in which the townspeople hold Grandet, it is clear that Eugenie's family is impoverished – as much emotionally as materially. Although the family is relatively well-to-do, Eugenie and her mother spend their mornings mending dusters in the same chairs, year in, year out, in an unheated house. They are unwitting of crucial facts of their existence: 'Eugenie and her mother knew nothing of Grandet's fortune. They valued the things of life only in the light of their vague conceptions and neither esteemed nor despised money, accustomed as they were to doing without it'. At first it isn't clear whether Eugenie and her mother refuse to take in the signs of their family's wealth, hence deny it, or whether they are simply incapable of absorbing its significance. This confusion seems to relate to the vagueness of all their feelings. In contrast to the scheming townspeople they live among, the narrator observes that the feelings of Eugenie and her mother were 'keen, though bruised without their realising it'; this, combined with their 'secret lives, made them strange

exceptions'. Eugenie, a daughter who has learned to do
without, is used to having her feelings bruised, and is her
father's only heir; hence she is an obvious target for those
around her. As the narrator notes, she is 'one of those birds,
unknowing victims of the high price paid on them' (p. 31).

Although Eugenie's devotion to her mother and her attraction to her cousin are plain, these are pale shadows of her
fascination with Grandet. Eugenie might well be pitied for
her mother's early death and her lover's flight, but pity would
be unsuited to the twisting emotions that bind this daughter
to her consuming father. She may want the best for her
mother, and desire every satisfaction from Charles, but what
she expects from her father is immeasurable. The guiding
question in this novel is not so much 'Who will Eugenie
Grandet marry?', the classic question of many realist novels;
rather it is 'Who will marry Eugenie Grandet?' Who will, in
marrying Eugenie, come between this daughter and this
father? Eugenie's fate, the eternal daughter, is to be married
– not to marry. Loyal to her father even after his death,
Eugenie would rather be chosen than to choose for herself.

Charles' first meeting with Eugenie, in a romantic sense,
had to be. In the wake of Eugenie's sheltered girlhood,
Charles was destined to appear. Nor is it chance that
Charles is effeminate, acute, and gentlemanly - not,
perhaps, such a contradiction. Charles evokes a far-off
Parisian sophistication, and a sensuality scorned by the
frugal Grandets – that is, everything his relatives are not. In
mind of the impression he hoped to make on arrival, 'he had
the idea of appearing there with the superiority of a fashionable young man, of driving the whole district to despair by
his display of luxury, of making his stay a memorable event,
and of introducing the innovations of Parisian life' (p. 35).
His appearance alerts Eugenie to qualities she would never
dare assume - vanity and ambition not least. Above all his
arrival in Saumur jolts her out of an acceptance of the way
things are, and interests her in the way things could – with a
little imagination – become. Because Charles possesses
these qualities in abundance, when they meet her undeveloped neutrality becomes obvious.

Eugenie is at a disadvantage in her affair with Charles
from the first; partly because she has spent twenty years in

a provincial backwater, but mostly because, during this time, she has lost touch with her imagination and sensuousness – qualities that might have strengthened her against his attractions. This makes her so vulnerable that she can only love a lover who is destined to leave her – the melancholic choice. As soon as her affair with Charles begins she has fantasies about their separation. At this level Charles' identity doesn't matter; rather his insignificance is crucial – as if the blanker he remains the more easily he can fit Eugenie's fantasies.

> Eugenie, who had never before seen a being of such perfection either in dress or person, thought that her cousin was a seraph from some heavenly region. With delight she breathed in the perfume exhaled by that head of hair which was so glossy and so gracefully curled. She would have liked to touch the white skin of those pretty kid gloves. She envied Charles his small hands, his complexion, the freshness and delicacy of his features. It is hardly possible to sum up the impression which the young dandy made on an ignorant girl, who spent all her time darning stockings and mending her father's clothes, and whose life had been spent in the shadow of that filthy wainscoting without seeing more than one passer-by an hour in the silent street outside. (p 38)

A strict upbringing often backfires, and so it does with Eugenie. The more concertedly Eugenie's parents ward against the kinds of excitement that might compromise Eugenie as a young girl, the less developed – the less sensitised – her relation to excitement and pleasure will be in later years.

While the plot of this novel is organised around who will marry Eugenie, the narrator probes a more subtle question, which is whether Eugenie's 'vague conceptions' of life are adequate. The moment Charles arrives Eugenie's dulled perceptions become alert, singular, and quick. Nothing escapes her; a keen-eyed neighbour notices how 'from time to time the young heiress stole a furtive glance at her cousin [with] a crescendo of astonishment and curiosity' (p. 34). This interest has a surprising effect; instead of setting Charles with his finery and breeding over and above herself, his grey uncultivated cousin, she immediately identifies with him. Rushing upstairs to prepare his room, she pushes her mother and family servant away, convinced that 'only she could appreciate her cousin's tastes and ideas' (p. 39). Charles' effect on Eugenie is electric – 'more ideas had rushed into her mind in a quarter of an hour than she had had since she was born' (p. 40).

Eugenie now enters a world quickened by self-interest, ambition, and envy. She sneaks into her cousin's room to watch him sleep, then she rushes out, embarrassed: 'She fled, both ashamed and happy at having come. Only innocence dares be so bold. Once it is no longer ignorant, Virtue can scheme as well as Vice' (p. 87). Within days she is crossing her parents. Alarmed at her daughter's indulgence of Charles, Madame Grandet asks 'What will your father say?' which Eugenie shrugs off with 'he won't notice' (p. 40). Her mother stands by, powerless, 'defenceless against the tones of her daughter's voice'. The narrator adds, 'Eugenie was sublime, she had become a woman' (p. 79). But what kind of woman has Eugenie become? One who has desires she expects will be met, or one who desires vicariously, through a lover who appears to her – miraculously enough – as a better version of herself? Why doesn't she try harder to keep her cousin's interest? Is it modesty that dampens her wishes? And, finally, to whom is she loyal? To existing authorities, her parents; or to her own desires, through which she might authorise herself?

By the time her father dies, Eugenie has become the kind of girl one might be warned against marrying. Drawn to harm the one she loves, she is a threat to any relationship. Sadly, and this is a sad novel, Eugenie takes the melancholic path: away from fulfilling her desires and toward negatively realising them. Why? Balzac's answer is simple. She becomes melancholic out of a mistaken sense of virtue: by doing what seems the right thing morally she ends up doing the wrong thing erotically. She experiences herself as not good enough for Charles, as unworthy of him, and hence unattractive. This leads her to feel divided from him and, more disconcertingly, from herself. The morning after his arrival, she stood before her bedroom mirror and 'experienced a tumultuous stirring of the heart. She got up again and again, stood before her mirror, and looked at herself like a conscientious author examining his own work critically and telling himself what is wrong with it' (p. 56). Imagining herself through his – more perfect – eyes, Eugenie dislikes what she sees: 'As she looked in the mirror, knowing as yet nothing of love, she said to herself, "I am too ugly; he won't take any notice of me"' (p. 57). In this way she loses sight of her attractiveness and becomes unlovely – a vulnerability her father and lover are quick to take advantage of.

This sequence can only repeat itself, leaving Eugenie – each time – further from fulfilment. And so everything goes on as before, with Eugenie secure in the knowledge that her life will end in the same place it began – in her parents' gloomy living room. This summary is glancing, yet it has resonance for every hysterical daughter. Eugenie's over-wrought apprehension of being left is, paradoxically, a guarantee of her abandonment. Her increasingly nervous state makes her unattractive to the cousin who excites her. Her fear of not having what it takes for her father and Charles to love her has a hand in their disappearances. Because of this fear she can only love a lover who is isn't there – which is why the moment her heart starts beating for Charles she has fantasies about their separation. Charles' identity doesn't matter, since his main role in her story is to realise her worst fear – that of being left.

Fearful of being found wanting Eugenie approaches her cousin cautiously, as if expecting rejection. She cannot see, as can the narrator, that her 'calm, glowing face, bordered with light like a pretty, newly opened flower, brought peace to the soul, communicated the charm of the pure conscience reflected in it, and arrested the eye' (p. 57). Rather than imagining what she and Charles may gain from being together – an eroticism not to be won separately – modesty tempers her imaginings. As the narrator remarks, 'modesty, or rather a fear of being unworthy, is one of the first virtues aroused by love'. And because she doesn't share her sense of unworthiness with anyone there is no way of remedying it. And so, instead of moving from a girlish naïvety to a womanly knowingness, Eugenie shifts sideways, from girlish ignorance to false – and depressed – modesty.

Eugenie doesn't fall in love with Charles so much as desire everything about him that reminds her of what she has lost sight of in herself. Plainly she is fascinated by his belongings, 'the pretty knick-knacks of his toilet equipment, his scissors and razors inlaid with gold', and by his 'head of hair which was so glossy and so gracefully curled'. And yet, except for a rush at their first meeting, she isn't drawn to him sexually – rather sensually. She lacks the confidence required for sexual interest: on discovering another woman in Charles's life – a 'great lady' from Paris – instead of feeling second best in Charles' affections, Eugenie vows to 'love him for ever'. Reading one of Charles' love letters to Annette 'her heart throbbed' while 'her feet were riveted to the spot'. The moment Eugenie identifies with Charles' desire for Annette, her affair becomes hysterical. In her fantasy she doesn't want Charles to love her, she wants to be Charles and so to love Annette in his place; to love Annette as passionately as she imagines Charles loves Annette.

This discovery comes just before Eugenie decides to give away her inheritance. Having identified with Charles in his affair with Annette, and hence understanding his need for wealth, Eugenie showers him with her gold. In offering Charles her gold coins, the narrator notes that 'she did not think of their rarity, nor of her father's mania, nor of the risk she ran in giving away a treasure so dear to his heart; no, she was thinking of her cousin'. She is so pleased at the thought of his pleasure that 'she clapped her hands in delight, like a child' (p. 114). Eugenie gets more out of giving her money away, especially power, than she ever got out of having it herself. Handing over her purse she says, 'Here are the savings of a poor girl who doesn't need anything'. In reversing her cousin's fortunes Eugenie momentarily experiences herself as valuable, even womanly. It is however profoundly ironic that a woman should feel bountiful, sexual, and generous at precisely the moment she gives away what is potentially valuable to her.

A strange calm falls over the house following this scene, with Grandet treating Eugenie and Charles as 'two children' for whom 'childhood and love were the same thing'. Balzac will spend the rest of the novel explaining how very different childhood and love really are; but first he lets his lovers enjoy their brief happiness. It soon becomes clear, however, that while Charles and Eugenie are in love, each loves differently – he with an eye to the future, she with her eyes shut to it. The death of his father pushes Charles both to accept looser links with others and the fact of there being limits to his freedom; he is as someone 'who had, as it were, reached the rock bottom of his sorrows and who, measuring the depth of the abyss into which he had fallen, had fully realised the difficulty of his future life' (p. 117). Eugenie, in contrast, 'abandoned herself deliciously to the current of love'. She doesn't however yield smoothly, she 'clutched at her happiness like a swimmer who clutches at a willow branch so that he can pull himself out of a river and rest on the bank' (p. 122). However deliciously love carries Eugenie off, life keeps pulling her back.

Eugenie's affair is lived in fantasy and so cannot last, of this Balzac is certain. Once Charles leaves for the West Indies, her happiness slowly dissolves. The difference between Charles, who throws off his sorrow to get on with life, and Eugenie, who takes sorrow into herself and identifies with it, is seen by the narrator as naturally occurring between the sexes:

> In every situation, women have more cause for grief than men and suffer more. A man has his strength and the exercise of his powers. He is active, he comes and goes, he is busy, he thinks, he plans for the future and finds consolation in it. That is what Charles did. But a woman stays at home; she remains face to face with her sorrow, with nothing to distract her from it; she plumbs the depths of the abyss it has opened up, and often fills it with her prayers and tears. That is what Eugenie did. (p. 134)

Man projects his negative feelings beyond himself, and in this way gets the better of bad experiences; woman remains within herself, absorbing feelings of loss which become the sum and limit of her experience. Eugenie's destiny is, then, 'to experience a woman's lot to the full, but without its consolations'. Balzac presents this (as perhaps it then seemed) as a function merely of gender: but now the issue must appear in a more complex light – we all know men whom this dynamic description mocks (and women who are admired for making the most of things).

Like father like daughter: Grandet and Eugenie block out the world around them. Grandet ignores his daughter's emerging womanhood, neglects his part in his brother's suicide, and is blind to his nephew's disdain. Eugenie refuses to absorb the messages that would upset her fantasy and, in disregarding them, becomes depressed. Her depression is however short-lived, since it quickly turns into melancholy once she recognises her own contribution to her ill fortune. With this shift – from feeling that she has lost what is important to her, to feeling that she has caused this loss – Eugenie's hands are tied.

Who then is responsible for Eugenie's melancholic turn? No-one directly, it seems. Her father may be a tyrant, but Eugenie's loyalty to him has the effect of making her, too, tyrannous. Nor is her mother to blame. Madame Grandet may die depressed, but she never complicates her depression by admiring her husband's power over her – as Eugenie admires her father's power over her. However this admiration doesn't last; when he becomes high-handed, Eugenie quickly turns on him. In contrast to her mother who dies in silence, Eugenie stands up to Grandet and proudly – loudly – identifies with his strength. But only for a moment. There is a twist: instead of appealing to her father for justice she appeals beyond him, to God the father – as if God's law might explain her subjection to a lawless father, more than her own feelings ever could.

Eugenie uses her religious fervour as a brace against her father, even though her piety supports the very family structure that fuels her conflict. When concerned friends visit, to ask Eugenie why she is being locked in her room, she replies, 'Gentlemen [...] I beg you not to concern yourselves with the matter. My father is master in his own house. As long as I live in this house, I must obey him. His conduct should not be subject to the approval or disapproval of other people; he is answerable only to God' (p. 152). Rather than challenge her father, Eugenie gives this responsibility to God, in the belief that He will protect her. The fact that God doesn't protect her is telling; perhaps because Balzac assumes that once you give up on yourself, others – God included – will too.

In old age Grandet becomes even more himself – more trenchant, self-important, and mercenary. The mutual dependence of father and daughter is clear; each is excited by the other, and uses the other to confirm a sense of themselves. Grandet, it transpires, locks Eugenie in her bedroom all the better to enjoy her:

> The next day, Grandet, following a habit he had adopted since Eugenie's imprisonment, took a few turns round his little garden. He had selected for his walk the moment when Eugenie was doing her hair. When the old man reached the big walnut tree, he would hide behind its trunk and stay for a few moments to look at his daughter's long tresses; he was no doubt wavering between the thoughts inspired by his temperamental obstinacy and the desire to embrace his child. (p. 153)

For her part, Eugenie chooses to 'look at her father out of the corner of her eye or watch him in her mirror'. Although Eugenie doesn't set up this situation, she gets something out of knowing she is vital to her father's pleasure. Neither can do without the other: Grandet needs his daughter to acknowledge – to prove – his importance, while Eugenie needs her father to make her feel valued. Moreover each is excited by a kind of pleasure – imaginative before it is real – that takes place at the edge of awareness. This puts Eugenie in loyal concert with her father, to the point that when she defies him she all the more strongly resembles him. Eugenie may be attracted to Charles, but it is her father – whose lust for gold mirrors her own devotion to Charles' treasures – who truly excites her.

Here the resemblance ends: whereas Eugenie is drawn to the sentimental value of Charles's treasures – his miniatures and dressing-case – Grandet is motivated by the market value of his gold. Eugenie looks after Charles' treasures as if they are a heartfelt gift; Grandet's gold is his booty, his secret treasure: 'the father and the daughter each coveted their fortunes, he so as to sell his gold, Eugenie to cast hers into an ocean of affection' (p. 114). Grandet sneaks into his chamber 'to cherish, caress, embrace, gloat over, glory in, his gold', while Eugenie privately fondles her 'new coins in mint condition, real works of art' – but neither fully appreciates what they have. Inevitably this affects their appreciation of each other; as if, under pressure of their own desires – Grandet for gold and Eugenie for sentiment – they lose sight of themselves and each other, without which appreciation is impossible.

As long as Eugenie can't appreciate what she has, she is tied to those who seem to. Before appreciation can happen she has to take imaginative hold of what is hers, and to prize it as hers; something which is only possible once she has

overcome her desire to receive love – and pleasure – child-
ishly. Because Eugenie is still bound up with early pleasures
– those of childhood – she experiences an imaginative all or
nothing: either she possesses everything of value, all her
parents' love, or she is entirely without it – and so without
value. Unable to face this question squarely Eugenie hoards
what is of value; as if, finding nowhere inside to keep it, she
has to keep it about her. This is why her fortune becomes
that much more valuable once she has given it away – and
made it real to herself. All part of a cycle in which, unable to
radiate her own sense of value, Eugenie is driven to uphold
the values of others.

Eugenie spends the seven years following Charles' departure in a daydream, her imagination carrying her off. A true
melancholic, she loves Charles freely once he isn't around:
'in short, her love was that solitary, genuine, lasting love
which pervades every thought and becomes the substance,
or, as our ancestors would have said, the stuff, of life'
(p. 135). Eugenie's love is frighteningly solitary, infertile, and
uncommunicative. But for someone for whom this represents love, the departure of the beloved, and his life with
another, is a sort of prerequisite. This daydream lasts until
New Year of 1819, when Grandet traditionally asks Eugenie
to show him her gold coins. Within just three days, the
narrator warns, 'a terrible drama would begin, a bourgeois
tragedy without poison, dagger, or bloodshed, but, as far as
the actors were concerned, more cruel than all the tragedies
enacted in the renowned house of Atreus' (p. 136). On
discovering Eugenie has given her gold to her cousin,
Grandet realises that he has not only lost a faithful
daughter, he has gained a rival – 'love had made Eugenie as
cunning as avarice had made her father'. Despite his rage –
'accursed serpent of a daughter!' – Grandet sees the situation truly, minus Eugenie's fond dreams. 'What's the good of
going to communion six times every three months', he asks
her, 'if you secretly give your father's gold to a good-for-
nothing who'll eat your heart out when you've only that left
to give him?' (p. 147). Grandet is able to see that Eugenie's
hopes are based not on what really happened, but on what
she really wanted to happen – appealing to her wishes and
not her memories. Had she appealed to her memories she

may not have become depressed; by reminding herself of what really happened, anger and disappointment would more readily follow than depression.

Grandet has enough insight into his daughter's feelings to take advantage of them. After his wife's death he plays on Eugenie's fear of being left should he die, and uses this fear to persuade her of the importance of miserliness; to the point that, confident of her loyal melancholy, he can prepare for death. Eugenie may never respect her father for his miserliness, yet she adopts it; and so is reconciled to a world that offers her little. It is as if, having given up on her own satisfaction, frustration takes its place; so that eventually she gets satisfaction from doing without. Instead of protesting against the suffering Charles causes her, she accepts it – almost embraces it. And so, through melancholy, she finally possesses him.

The death of her parents may explain Eugenie's sadness, but not her melancholy – which anyway appears well before Grandet dies. Left by a mother who 'pitied Eugenie for having to go on living', and a father whose last request is to 'put some gold in front of me', Eugenie is at last alone. She is quickly the subject of town gossip: 'Mademoiselle Grandet's profound melancholy was a secret to no-one. But though everyone had an idea of the cause, she never uttered a word which might justify the suspicions entertained by all social circles in Saumur about the state of the rich heiress' heart' (p. 164). In contrast to the sharp-tongued locals, the narrator's response to Eugenie's plight is sympathetic, seeing in it a reflection of her long deprivation of intimacy.

> In the life of the spirit, as in that of the body, there is a breathing-in and a breathing-out; the soul needs to absorb the feelings of another soul, to assimilate them, to return them enriched. Without that wonderful human phenomenon, there is no life for the heart; it suffers from lack of air and fades away. (p. 169)

Without vital contact with others Eugenie fades away, falls silent. This is the deathly outcome of Eugenie's form of renunciatory love. Having failed to mourn the people important to her, their memories are never put to rest; nor does anyone near encourage her to. The consequences are profound; she never makes a clear distinction between the past and the present, the dead and the living. While outwardly she accepts her parents' death, she remains within their influence, preferring to keep their protection than to cast off their authority. She would, it seems, rather be under her dead father's thumb than be without any pressure above her.

This is a heroine who would rather devote herself to upholding the dead than risk doing away with them. To do away with her father's presence Eugenie would have to use some of the inner force that she has, as Grandet's daughter, derived from him. Because she holds back from doing this, she is – paradoxically – without the strength which might free her of Grandet's influence. Instead her strong feelings are given over to melancholy, thus isolating them from feelings which may otherwise soften them. She withdraws from the world, adopting a charitable manner which demands nothing more of her than an easy generosity that, having inherited, she can well afford.

This is the point at which Eugenie dies – imaginatively at least. Having turned away from the crushed hopes of her mother, and the mercantile ambitions of her father and worldly cousin, she is without inspiration. As long as she lives in a world with no more certain pleasure than melancholy, she has no real incentive for overcoming it. At the end of this novel it isn't just the heroine who despairs of hope, the narrator too leaves off his pen after a generalising sweep which distances Eugenie from him. Eugenie is no longer a particular woman, subject to specific conditions and pressures, she has become a type, almost an embarrassment.

Although Eugenie marries before the novel closes, it is less to fulfil her erotic hopes than to stem them forever. Within her chaste marriage Eugenie takes out on her husband what she was unable to take out on her father: she kills her husband, in spirit if not in deed, by refusing to live up to his love for her. Pushed to destroy their relationship with a part of herself she herself doesn't recognise, she causes him – along with his love – to disappear. Women like Madame de Bonfons, as Eugenie becomes, give marriage a bad name; she uses it to define herself negatively and to put herself off limits – not to discover love's fullness. Her husband endures marriage to a woman who, opposed to her own eroticism, disdains their tie. Having opened the novel with Eugenie a princess, Balzac closes it with his heroine a stale queen. Her first erotic rush of feeling – 'more ideas had rushed into her mind in a quarter of an hour than she had had since she was born' – is now reversed. She sees 'her whole destiny at a glance. All that was left to her was to unfold her wings, reach out to heaven, and live in prayer until the day of her deliverance' (p. 181).

Eugenie Grandet leaves many readers feeling flat and pessimistic. Why? Could it be that it is dispiriting to identify with a character who fails to respond to life positively, and who lets herself be compromised by it – seemingly so easily? Or is it that Eugenie plays on the reader's own vulnerabilities, so that sympathy for her brings with it visions of one's own downward spiral? Perhaps Eugenie Grandet's story is disturbing because it slides from – momentary – hysteria, to depression, and on to melancholia. This downward spiral isn't explained by the death of her parents or the betrayal of her lover; although these events put pressure on her, in the end she chooses her own fate. It is Eugenie who decides not to give imaginative space to her father and lover, blocking them from her awareness. Moreover by telling Charles that she is 'a poor girl who doesn't need anything', and in letting her father do whatever he likes with her mother's fortune, Eugenie refuses to credit her own value. She would rather stay in the position of wanting nothing, than accept the potential for disappointment that wanting brings with it.

Note

1. Honore de Balzac, *Eugenie Grandet*, translated by Sylvia Raphael (OUP, 1990) pp. 85–86. Further page numbers are given in brackets in the text.

3

'My nerves disdained hysteria': Charlotte Brontë's *Villette*

What would have happened if Eugenie Grandet had told her own story, if there had been no narrator to tell it for her? How knowingly, how expansively, would she have described her life? How keen would she have been to understand it from another point of view? Would she have forgotten certain episodes, or ruled others out as too slight? Balzac's heroines have lives which, however intriguing, the narrator can articulate; in contrast, Brontë's heroines – who double as narrators – have lives which defy elaboration. Whereas Balzac eagerly explored heroines distinct from himself, Charlotte Brontë saw the novel as a veiled form of autobiography. Lucy Snowe, the heroine in *Villette*, is wary of the world she finds herself in and withholds her trust from others. The story Lucy tells, of her stay in a Belgium school, is the one she is willing to tell; however, because she takes flight from aspects of this experience, her story is not to be trusted. And whereas Balzac's narrator is keen for the reader to know everything about Eugenie, apologising when he falls short of this, Lucy Snowe keeps a tight hand on her narrative, never admitting her evasions.

Balzac believed that if you looked at someone long and hard enough they would open themselves to you; Charlotte Brontë was less optimistic. Both authors assume that understanding another involves exploring his (or her) mind, however Brontë was less confident of the success of this. In an early letter, she refers to the minds of others as 'sealed volumes', each of which has a 'hidden language, whose turnings, windings, inconsistencies, and obscurities, so frequently baffle the researches of the honest observer of human nature'.[1] Because something about our mental life evades the honest observer, Brontë recommends that we follow the inner workings of the mind, however peculiar – and occasionally lying – these may be. This is what happens in *Villette*, in which Lucy appears to tell of her experiences in Belgium, but actually relates her experience of her own – highly idiosyncratic – mind.

Villette, like *Jane Eyre*, presents the life of a woman who is poor, plain, and orphaned. The story, told through Lucy Snowe's eyes, tells of her journey to Belgium to find independence and love. However Lucy Snowe is fundamentally different from Jane Eyre, being without passion, certainty, and spontaneity – and instead being reserved in all things. She is particularly taken aback by the love that those around her display and take for granted, and from which she feels excluded. Whatever happiness Lucy finds is in snatches, and can never be taken hold of; although, by the end of the novel she has made peace with her pilgrimage through life.

The novel is based on Charlotte Brontë's experiences in Brussels – renamed Villette – and has at its heart an intense pupil-teacher relationship. After her voyage to Europe Lucy finds a post as a teacher in a girls' school, where she wins the respect of the capable but manipulative headmistress, Madame Beck, and slowly gains authority over the unruly girls. Lucy also becomes deeply attached to John Bretton, the school doctor, recognising him as a companion from childhood (one unlikely coincidence among many); with pained interest she watches Dr John flirt with Ginevra Fanshawe and then successfully court Paulina Home. Although the plot relies on supernatural incidents, these are all given realistic explanations and serve mainly to highlight Lucy's nervous isolation. Eventually Lucy's interests turn to the tyrannical yet kind Professor Paul Emmanuel, a cousin of Madame Beck, whose attitude to Lucy slowly changes from irritability to esteem. Through his generosity she opens a school, at the same time as he is sent off by his family to do business in the West Indies. The ending is uncertain, leaving it open whether the professor's ship returns or is wrecked at sea.

In this novel Brontë explores the idea, through her heroine, that the refusal to express certain emotional and sexual truths is really a kind of knowing. This is a point which Freud was later to put. Lucy Snowe hides the facts of her life – her loneliness and need for love – however much they make her suffer, until she is in a position to absorb them. This takes time, and until this happens there is little she can do to resolve her conflict. She appears to understand that before she can let these facts back into awareness something important must occur: most importantly, that any gaps in understanding around the hidden facts of her life should be filled. This is why Brontë follows the workings of Lucy's mind so painstakingly, attending to what she doesn't say behind all that she does.

It would be easy to say of *Villette*, and many readers do, that Lucy Snowe is a liar: however this is mistaken. Lucy Snowe appears deceitful because her story baffles: a nun swoops down on her out walking, hysterical laughter wafts down corridors, letters are stolen and then reappear, keys are quietly pocketed, and surveillance is openly practised. These seem calculated to make the reader suspicious; yet this is not the same as saying that Lucy Snowe is self-consciously deceiving others – perhaps it is herself she deceives and we pick up on this through oddities of her narrative. Lucy never actually lies about her past, nor does she tell her story otherwise than it is, but she does withhold essential aspects of it. If Lucy is not to be trusted as a narrator, nor – it seems – is the world she inhabits. Distrust, in the world as she finds it, breeds distrust.

This novel unsettles, just as it intrigues and frustrates, not because the narrator sets out to unnerve the reader, but because the experiences she has are unnerving. Some critics have read *Villette* as a gothic tale, others as a psychological fantasy – why not simply as a story subject to the distortions of the teller? Despite her withholding Lucy is an acute heroine. Of all the heroines I discuss she is the best educated; adept in foreign languages, she is familiar with a range of literature, scriptures, and classics. Above all she is psychologically knowing and skilled at handling others. All these abilities prove useful during her travels. On arriving at the boarding school, alone and at night, with a scrappy reference, she is grateful to be offered a post as governess to the headmistress' children. This immediately puts her among women as canny as herself – teachers mainly – in an atmosphere of feverish excitement. Shortly after settling in, Lucy runs into a friend in the town whom she'd been envious of when they were children. Now a cultivated young woman, still protected by her wealthy father, Paulina is as attractive to Lucy as ever. These two women, the stern head-mistress Madame Beck and the innocent Paulina Bretton, quickly become the focus of Lucy's imaginative life: although she is drawn to Graham Bretton and Monsieur Paul, it is these two women who really excite her.

Apart from a summer holiday, when a creeping loneliness makes her ill, Lucy's struggles never take an outward shape. She continues to have a grip on reality even while exaggerating and distorting it. Her unspoken fear, which lies behind her urge to distort, appears to be less what others might do to her – to persecute her, for instance – than what they might *fail* to do – that is, let her down. As it turns out this heroine's greatest fear, and most elaborate fantasy, is based on her anxiety of being overlooked. This explains her need – almost craving – for others; as if only through others can she confirm who she is. To the point that, when others actually do let her down, she has fantasies of her own disappearance.

What is striking about Lucy is her inner precariousness, as compared with her steely outward manner. She doesn't seem to realise that the vulnerability which draws others to her and makes her interesting to them is what she disdains in herself. This steely manner, which well conceals a softer centre, is fairly common in women. Like many women, Lucy assumes that she needs to guard against others, and so keeps them at arm's length. As a result she organises her life around imagined fears, rather than creating a life independent of them.

Lucy's need to control her experience, as opposed to letting it find its own shape, has an important function: it protects her from the possibility of breakdown. We are never told what is so frightening that it requires her constant guard, but it appears to have early origins. The closest she gets to describing it is in a vision which follows a childhood holiday with her godmother:

> I will permit the reader to picture me, for the next eight years, as a bark slumbering through halcyon weather, in a harbour still as glass – the steersman stretched on the little deck, his face up to heaven, his eyes closed: buried, if you will, in a long prayer. A great many women and girls are supposed to pass their lives something in that fashion; why not I with the rest?[2]

She then upsets expectations, by turning this sentimental vision into a nightmare:

> Picture me then idle, basking, plump, and happy, stretched on a cushioned deck, warmed with constant sunshine, rocked by breezes indolently soft. However, it cannot be concealed that, in that case, I must somehow have fallen over-board, or that there must have been wreck at last. I too well remember a time – a long time, of cold, of danger, of contention. To this hour, when I have the nightmare, it repeats the rush and saltness of briny waves in my throat, and their icy pressure on my lungs. I even know there was a storm, and that not of one hour nor one day. For many days and nights neither sun nor stars appeared; we cast with our own hands the tackling out of the ship; a heavy tempest lay on us; all hope that we should be saved was taken away. In fine, the ship was lost, the crew perished. (p. 94)

This is autobiography of a peculiar kind, with a romantic childhood vision turning into an imaginative extreme that requires a nightmare to contain it. There is no trace of the experience which triggered it; that something awful has happened – at least in fantasy – is clear, but no more. Except that, although Lucy has survived it, clearly she suffers its effects.

Charlotte Brontë appears less interested in representing experience realistically, than in communicating hidden truths. She dismissed writers like Jane Austen for a style 'more real than true' – truer to reality than to imagination – preferring to bring out the particularity, the strangeness, of mental life. Lucy Snowe shares this preference; she would rather explore emotional complexities than reflect reality evenly. 'I always liked to penetrate to the real truth', Lucy admits, 'I liked seeking the goddess in her temple, and handling the veil, and daring the dread glance'. However to seek the truth isn't always to comprehend it, just as to face one's fears isn't always to understand them. Is Lucy in a position to understand her experience? Or would she rather keep quiet about certain experiences, vaguely alluding to them in fantasy? In other words, is Lucy Snowe able to represent her experiences, even when they verge on the hysterical; or is she, by virtue of experiencing their effects, unable to write about them?

Certainly the story Lucy Snowe tells assumes an emotionally heightened landscape. The plot winds and twists, as if she – as narrator – is avoiding unwelcome truths. Lucy's curiosity drives the story forward, until something blocks it, stemming her curiosity. What exactly is the memory Lucy is drawn to, yet wary of? One answer seems to be biographical. *Villette* was inspired by two visits Charlotte Brontë made to Brussels to teach in the 1840s. Having accepted the need for her sisters and herself to earn a living, Charlotte planned to open her own school in Yorkshire. Her trips abroad were partly to find out how to run a school, partly to spend time away from a family afflicted by illness and death, and partly to avoid becoming a country governess. After an initial trip with her sister Charlotte made her second trip alone, in the quiet hope of getting a certain professor's attention. This professor, a married man, humiliated Charlotte on her return to England by ignoring her increasingly impassioned letters to him – written prior to beginning *Villette*. Although these biographical details don't account for the power of *Villette*, which stands in its own creative right, they do explain something of its extraordinary intensity, and especially those moments – hinted at but never described – which Lucy leaves out of her story. There is something the heroine either can't or won't say, around which the novel turns. Rather than an experience she can't remember, it appears to be something which never actually happened – which yet, in fantasy, should have happened, which is why she keeps returning to it.

Whatever other genres *Villette* satisfies – gothic drama, veiled autobiography, hysterical narrative – it is above all a romance. It isn't, however, about love in any simple sense. For Lucy Snowe love is unmentionable; a feeling to be fought for but never declared, much less taken for granted. She describes herself as being totally without family, with no relatives to love or depend on. Following her nightmare about the storm at sea, she writes, 'As far as I recollect, I complained to no-one about these troubles. Indeed, to whom could I complain?' And again, 'there remained no possibility of dependence on others; to myself alone could I look'. This heroine's seeming independence is never far from isolation; on setting sail for Europe, without friends, destination, or money, she is like a missionary – but without a mission. Here lies an odd tension between real life and fiction, which is that what might have been for Charlotte a chance to win the man and career she longs for, becomes, transposed into fiction, Lucy's fraught journey into the unknown. And yet we know from a letter, written soon after Charlotte's return from Belgium, that she felt a strong wish to return to something familiar. 'I returned to Brussels', she confesses to a friend, 'after Aunt's death against my conscience – prompted by what then seemed an irresistible impulse'.[3] Charlotte may have decided to return to the school for professional reasons, but her 'irresistible impulse' suggests an emotional pull.

The power of *Villette* is explained by the presence of reminiscences which have yet to be turned into memories – that are still so full of feeling that they won't settle into a stream of memories. By returning to Brussels a third time, this time in fiction, Brontë tells a story that should – in fantasy – have happened on her second visit. There is then good reason why *Villette* is tense and oblique; there is too much at risk for the heroine to tell her story otherwise. At the heart of the story is an intensely personal confession about Lucy's need to be loved by a man she idealises. A novel full of letters, *Villette* is finally the letter Charlotte Brontë couldn't send her professor, full of imaginative flights and feelings evoked by her journey, an embroidering of her real experience.

When Charlotte Brontë wrote *Villette* she was engaged in reminiscing. The aim of reminiscence, as opposed to memory, is to find words for fantasies and feelings which can then become subject to memory. *Villette* is a work of reminiscence, one which brings together stray memories, intricate fantasies, and undeveloped feelings with the aim of making them meaningful. While Lucy recalls certain events vividly, she passes over others – often more central – entirely. We know that it is reminiscence rather than memory that drives her story on because Lucy is compelled to return again and again to the same images, as if she hasn't captured what is most telling about them. At the core of *Villette* are reminiscences which evade Lucy's attempts to remember them: the fact that ultimately she fails, doesn't make her deceiving or lying – rather it reflects the difficulty of her task.

By visiting Brussels once more, this time in fiction, Charlotte Brontë was able to untangle some of the feelings which disturbed her memory of earlier trips. However, as borne out by the matted story of *Villette*, no creative act can dissolve the hysterical structure which tangled her feelings in the first place. No act of writing, however creative, can do this. Charlotte wrote in private, in the absence of the professor on to whom her intense appeal was directed – and so never diffused. Nonetheless, even though Brontë's attempt to resolve her relation to the professor by writing a novel about it failed, the act of writing may well have relieved much of the conflict it aroused.

It is at first unclear why, when someone starts reminiscing, their imagination doesn't turn the memories which inspire it into pleasurable ones. Why, one wonders, didn't Charlotte Brontë write a novel in which the heroine wins the professor away from his wife, instead of one in which she fails to? Why replace a happy ending – written at her father's insistence for the first edition – with a dark, enigmatic ending for the second edition? Why did Charlotte choose to frustrate rather than fulfil her heroine? Not, one presumes, because she wanted to beat Lucy with the same stick that she herself had felt. It is psychologically more likely that, before Charlotte's deepest wishes could be fulfilled, the anxiety which blocked them had to be dealt with – 'bound', as Freud put it. All the dreams, hallucinations, overheard conversations, and absences of Lucy Snowe's story required a fuller expression than she first gives them. It is only when Lucy's reminiscences stop making her anxious that they – slowly – become memories agreeable enough to be elaborated without being broken off from.

In the early stages of her journey Lucy is undecided about the direction she is going in, and repeatedly asks herself, 'Will you go forward or backward?' Whereas going forward means facing her wishes head on and finding ways to realise them, going backward means falling prey to these same wishes in another form – as fantasies, fears, or hallucinations. At each impasse Lucy is powerfully tempted to cease all movement, presumably in the hope that by not going forward or backward her conflicts will also cease. However Lucy's attempt to take flight inevitably fails. *Villette* reflects this tension; occasional passages are themselves in flight, to or from what is never clear, while at other points her story nearly stops, as if the effort of telling it is suddenly too great, and language inadequate to it. It is hardly a coincidence that the boatman who rows Lucy over to her ship is called Charon, and that her bawdy stewardess greets her with hysterical laughter.

Lucy may guard her solitude fiercely, but she also longs for someone to break it. While teachers and girls form close huddles, Lucy stalks draughty corridors or risks bad weather. In an important sense Lucy's estrangement is chosen; she is so bent on observing others that she has little interest in friendship. She keeps an eye on whoever she is with, as if to maintain a sense of herself as distinct from them. Without a sense of her difference from others she appears in danger of disappearing – imaginatively – altogether. While she prides herself on the way she watches others – 'unobserved I could observe' – at the same time she dreads being overlooked by them. As she admits to her professor, 'it kills me to be forgotten, Monsieur' (p. 699).

While the recognition of others is essential to one's identity, Lucy's need goes deeper than this: she depends on the recognition of others for her inner sense of self – out of which identity springs. Lucy's ultimate vulnerability – as expressed in her breakdown during the holidays – is that, left alone, she will die, imaginatively if not physically.

Madame Beck is quick to see the vulnerability behind Lucy's steeliness, and to take advantage of both. Although active in the school, Madame Beck is largely a creation of Lucy's imagination. 'Wise, firm, faithless; secret, crafty, passionless; watchful and inscrutable; acute and insensate – withal perfectly decorous – what more could be desired?' Surely this better describes an aspect of the mind, the conscience, than a woman's personality? From the moment they meet, Madame Beck watches, supervises, and restrains Lucy in the most powerful way – through suggestion. These two may be the only ones to know it, but they are evenly matched. Just as Madame Beck is alive to Lucy's untapped strength, Lucy is an able critic of her employer: 'she did not wear a woman's aspect, but rather a man's. Power of a particular kind strongly limned itself in all her traits, and that power was not *my* kind of power'. This opposition clearly excites Lucy, who feels 'as if a challenge of strength between opposing gifts was given' (p. 141). Her first lesson, a simple one, is that one's strongest wishes must be matched by a willingness to go after them. ' "Will you," said Madame Beck, "go backward or forward?" indicating with her hand, first, the small door of communication with the dwelling-house, and then the great double portals of the classes or schoolrooms' (p. 141). If Lucy wishes to be more than a governess, she must overcome her timidity about her ambition to teach – this is what her first lesson teaches her.

Madame Beck's lesson in ambition is quite different from the lessons in survival that women have previously taught Lucy. The headmistress counsels that it isn't enough for Lucy to wish for distinction; if she is to achieve it she must act on her wishes. Lucy's equivocation about going backward or forward turns out to be fundamental. Will she continue to project her satisfactions on to others, only realising them vicariously? Or will she fulfil her wishes, disregarding their impact on others? In contrast to Lucy's sensitiveness to the opinion of others, Madame Beck couldn't care less what others think of her. The whole school knows that she secretly goes through their belongings and that she dismisses staff on flimsy grounds, but this doesn't bother her. Determined to master her world, she refuses to be compromised by it. While Lucy can't help admiring the way her employer takes her success for granted, and exercises her authority freely, she despairs of ever being like her.

Lucy learns from Madame Beck the advantages of being inscrutable, and of pursuing one's wishes single-mindedly. Because Madame Beck doesn't mind what others think of her, she can afford to be cool and occasionally unpleasant. She demonstrates to Lucy that there is something worse than losing another's love, which is losing their respect. Respect is something that is won or lost within a relationship of intimacy; it is wrested from another, often after a struggle. Lucy sees this struggle in Madame Beck's courtship with Monsieur Paul, and despite herself is drawn into it, fascinated by it. Unlike Madame Beck, who doesn't consider reprisal when she acts, Lucy lives in constant fear of it. Ashamed to make her wishes known to herself, much less tell others, Lucy shrinks from contact with loved ones in fantasy. Her main dread takes the form of harming a loved one, of losing people dear to her: the more she pushes this out of awareness, the more strongly she fears their loss.

Lucy Snowe's demand to be loved hasn't escaped critics of *Villette*, some of whom were openly critical of it. Harriet Martineau expressed her concern in a newspaper review of 1853:

> All the female characters, in all their thoughts and lives, are full of one thing, or are regarded by the reader in the light of that one thought – love. It begins with the child of six years old, at the opening – a charming picture – and it closes with it at the last page; and so dominant is this idea – so incessant is the writer's tendency to describe the need of being loved – that the heroine, who tells her own story, leaves the reader at last under the uncomfortable impression of her having either entertained a double love, or allowed one to supersede another without notification of the transition.[4]

The heroine's need to be loved, starting in childhood and lasting into womanhood, upsets this critic. It also upsets

Lucy, who prefers to perceive it in people around her rather than herself. When Lucy meets Paulina Bretton, apparently by chance after some years, she is struck by how attractive her friend is. Lucy interprets the clear features of her young friend as proof that life has been kind to her because safe-guarded by love: 'Her eyes were the eyes of one who can remember; one whose childhood does not fade like a dream, nor whose youth vanishes like a sunbeam' (p. 359). 'She would not take life', Lucy continues, 'loosely and incoher-ently, in parts, and let one season slip as she entered on another: she would retain and add; often review from the commencement, and so grow in harmony and consistency as she grew in years' (p. 360). In contrast to the shipwreck which Lucy uses to describe her own early life, Paulina appears – to Lucy's projective eye – enhanced and unharmed by experience.

Paulina says aloud what Lucy herself would never dare: 'Lived and loved!' said Paulina, 'is that the summit of earthly happiness, the end of life – to love'. She pauses, correcting herself, 'If Schiller had said to *be* loved – he might have come nearer the truth, is that not another thing, Lucy, to be loved?' (p. 389). This is a hope Lucy cannot share: instead she envies Paulina what she herself never had – the chance to experience her feelings without analysing them first. Paulina's seamless memory, her easy assumption that she will be loved, and her wide-eyed sense of the future, are too much for Lucy. Cut off from these hopes in herself, Lucy projects them on to those she feels affinity with. However what she doesn't realise is that by seeing in Madame Beck, Paulina, and Monsieur Paul the potentials she would like for herself, she ties herself to them with invisible strings. Fooling others with her independent manner, Lucy's true desires – not least her disguised rage for dependence – go unnoticed.

This heroine's dilemma is less whether to confide in others, than whether to relate to them at all. And yet she longs for her isolation to end: 'Is there nothing more for me in life', she asks herself, 'no true home – nothing to be dearer to me than myself, and by its paramount preciousness to draw from me better things than I care to culture for myself only?' (p. 450). Her longing is for a self greater than a sum of its parts, for a life beyond personal interest and self-defence. Thus she envies Paulina, who moves easily from her feelings to her thoughts and then back again, and who acts on her wishes spontaneously. Above all she envies Paulina her belief that it is only a matter of time before the good things she longs for are hers.

Lucy's fear of not being able to please others seems linked, at a deep level, with her fear of not being able to please herself. Instead of opening herself to erotic feelings, she squashes them. On falling in love with Graham Bretton, she goes into thrilling details of her feelings: 'my longing', she writes, 'and all of a similar kind, it was necessary to knock on the head; which I did, figuratively, after the manner of Jael to Sisera, driving a nail through their temples. Unlike Sisera, they did not die: they were but tran- siently stunned, and at intervals would turn on the nail with a rebellious wrench; then did the temples bleed, and the brain thrill to its core' (p. 176). In this scene Lucy murders her sexual feelings because they clash with her sense of propriety. Throughout this novel Responsibility, Duty, and Common-sense appear in upper-case – these are the nails she drives through her longings. They may look like ideals, except that ideals are never as imperious and unnegotiable as these. She herself admits, 'I have ever felt most burden- some that sort of sensibility which bends of its own will, a giant slave under the sway of good sense' (p. 71). This good sense that Lucy bends under is a law to itself, more a compulsion than a standard. As long as she experiences good sense as a force opposing her own interests, she remains at war with herself.

Although Lucy openly wars with Monsieur Paul, the Catholic literature master, her real struggle is with Madame Beck: 'She was *my* rival, heart and soul, though secretly, under the smoothest bearing, and utterly unknown to all save her and myself' (p. 544). Lucy's wish to rival Madame Beck in her relationship with Monsieur Paul is what finally pushes her conflict outside herself – and thus she becomes openly hysterical. On the simplest level Lucy wants Monsieur Paul so that Madame Beck can't have him. This desire gives Lucy considerable insight into her rival: 'Deep into some of Madame's secrets I had entered – I know not

how; by an intuition or an inspiration which came to me – I
know not whence' (p. 544). As the tables turn, it is no longer
the headmistress who keeps her eye on Lucy, but Lucy who
watches Madame Beck. Lucy aspires to a womanly position,
but on the sly, as if to avoid openly identifying with the
headmistress. This leads her to a paradoxical – yet typically
hysterical – situation, which is that while she respects
Madame Beck as a mentor, she dissociates from her as a
woman. This leads her to perceive Madame Beck as stripped
of womanliness; as terse, even mannish – anything but a
powerful rival.

Again and again Lucy chooses solitude, despite this
opening her to strong impulses which – in extreme moments
– become terrible visions. Having accepted a post which
involves being left alone, she then experiences this as an
attack on herself – by who or what is never clear. The climax
comes in the summer vacation when she stays at school
with sole care of a handicapped child. As the child's fever
rages and a storm breaks, Lucy breaks down. But before she
does, true to her privational – even messianic – nature, she
warms to her struggle:

> With what dread force the conviction would grasp me that Fate
> was my permanent foe, never to be conciliated. I did not, in my
> heart, arraign the mercy or justice of God for this; I concluded it
> to be part of his great plan that some must suffer deeply while
> they live, and I thrilled in the certainty that of this number, I
> was one. (p. 229)

Lucy has been chosen to suffer, while those around her live
freely; however this singularity proves too much and she
collapses under the strain.

Unable to distinguish between the outside world and her
inner world, Lucy starts seeing things. The worst of it is
captured in a dream which doesn't fade on waking: 'Meth-
ought the well-loved dead, who had loved *me* well in life, met
me elsewhere, alienated'. Lucy's longing is so great – and her
reluctance to confess it so strong – that loved ones return to
haunt her, unloving and aloof. Instead of the anger she
might have felt at being abandoned, she feels got at and
persecuted. In the same nightmare she recalls, in purple
prose, that 'quite unendurable was the pitiless and haughty
voice in which Death challenged me to engage his unknown

terrors' (pp. 231–2). With this Lucy is pushed out of the school and into the rain; as if only after confronting the worst of her fears can her recovery begin. Eventually she faints outside a Catholic church and wakes at the feet of a priest – hinting at her surrender to God the father.

Lucy's fever runs for days, after which her story picks up again with a rush. She wakes in her godmother's house, disconcerted yet pleased to be surrounded by familiar things. Her convalescence is long; not least because Dr John, Mrs Bretton's son, is in charge of it. His diagnosis is 'a case of spectral illusion . . . resulting from long-continued mental conflict'. Lucy's problem, according to his medical training, is untreatable: 'medicine can give nobody good spirits', he tells her. 'My art halts at the threshold of Hypochondria: she just looks in and sees a chamber of torture, but can neither say nor do much' (p. 257). When it comes to healing the split which underlies her collapse, Lucy is on her own.

> The divorced mates – Spirit and Substance – were hard to re-unite: they greeted each other, not in an embrace, but a racking sort of struggle. The returning sense of sight came upon me, red, as if it swam in blood; suspended hearing rushed back loud, like thunder; consciousness revived in fear; I sat up appalled, wondering into what region, amongst what strange beings I was waking. (p. 237)

Once Lucy does wake, it isn't to a self she recognises: 'I should have understood what we call a ghost, as well as I did the commonest object' (p. 237). Slowly this strangeness dissolves, but without entirely leaving her. Her godmother, in particular, continues to be oddly unsettling:

> the difference between her and me might be figured by that between the stately ship, cruising on a smooth sea with its full complement of crew, a captain gay and brave, and venturous and provident; and the life-boat, which most days of the year lies dry and solitary in an old, dark boat-house, only putting to sea when the billows run high in rough weather, when cloud encounters water, when danger and death divide between them the rule of the great deep. (p. 254)

For all the comfort around her, knowing it belongs to others keeps Lucy alert to 'the rule of the great deep'.

As the story continues, more smoothly now, Lucy has the task of reconciling the two sides of herself – the reasonable and the imaginative. Clearly her loyalty to reason and common sense is divided: 'Reason is vindictive as a devil: for me, she was always envenomed as a step-mother. If I have obeyed her it has chiefly been with the obedience of fear, not of love' (p. 308). Lucy's reasonableness is based on fear; she concedes to reason, respects its power, but never embraces it. Rather than bowing to reason, Lucy's recovery depends on strengthening her ties to her imagination – 'that softer power'. To bring this about she must loosen the hold that conscience – masked as reason – has over her. Rather than falling in with a harsh conscience, she needs to develop her imagination to withstand harshness.

An imaginative revival doesn't happen by itself, nor quickly. Lucy has to fight for it – she has to want it. Crucially she can't make it happen on her own; she needs help to relax her exacting conscience. This is what Monsieur Paul does, urging her, with friendly prodding, to overcome her reserve and to foster less developed aspects of herself. He persuades her to act a foppish man in the school panto-mime, to show off her intellect in front of his colleagues and, above all, he gives her courage – and motivation – to release herself from the hold Madame Beck has over her. None of this happens swiftly, and even when it does it is in fits and starts: characteristically she takes a step forward and then stands to one side, as if the step taken wasn't hers. This makes an impression on the narrative itself, which is at one moment bold and the next reticent, in sympathy with Lucy's shifting moods.

Monsieur Paul's encouragement allows Lucy to see her longing for Dr Graham for what it is – an infatuation. He offers her another pair of eyes to see herself through, giving her a much needed perspective. He also gets her to accept that her fixation with the mysterious nun who sweeps down when she is out walking as just that – a fixation. Above all their friendship pierces her loneliness. Lost in thought, Lucy catches sight of him through a window: 'a cap-tassel, a brow, two eyes filled a pane of that window; the fixed gaze of those two eyes hit right against my own glance: they were watching me. I had not till that moment known that tears were on my cheek, but I felt them now' (p. 310). Monsieur Paul watches Lucy as closely as the headmistress, but with a different aim: not to expose her vulnerability and resistance, as Madame Beck does, but to reveal potentials that, previously, had felt too precious to share.

Although Monsieur Paul is more eccentric than Lucy, and has every reason to question his own place in the world, he encourages Lucy to feel that her own place is secure. His support could be interpreted – and often is by feminist critics – as patronising. But is it really? Apart from being occasionally chauvinistic and teasing, Monsieur Paul is the only person who cares for Lucy in a disinterested way. Through him she can own up to her sadness as sadness, and not bitterness. His influence helps Lucy to develop more enduring and expansive qualities than her initial precariousness afforded.

In addition, Monsieur Paul gets Lucy to see how little reality has to do with her more extreme states of mind. He helps her to see how much resistance and longing have divided her, thus easing her experience of both. This makes her better at recognising her own distress, as opposed to appealing to someone who may relieve it – so that she can feel inconsolable without needing someone to articulate it for her. Hence Lucy continues to feel her loneliness as neglect, but no longer as an attack on herself. Best of all, Monsieur Paul frees her to act on her own behalf, rather than expecting others to act for her. Through their relationship she comes to see herself in a less divided way, discovering a more expansive self than the one modelled by Madame Beck.

And yet the professor's influence is not miraculous. Important decisions still remain for Lucy to make; crucially, whether she will approach the world in a forward or backward-seeking way. Will she remain in an unsatisfactory but safe present, or step into an exciting hence risky future? At various moments Lucy uses the full moon to symbolise the ambitions she projects on to others, as distinct from the half-moon she keeps for herself. 'I suppose, Lucy Snowe', the narrator asks, 'the orb of your life is not to be so rounded; for you the crescent-phase must suffice' (p. 451). And yet this half moon won't suffice; if Lucy is to move forward she needs to make her demands explicit, thus

opening herself to success, failure, and rejection. In particular, if she is to discover the secret of Monsieur Paul's first
love, a nun who died tragically young, she can't stay in the
role of observer. 'Was I, then, to be frightened by Justine
Marie? Was the picture of a pale dead nun to rise, an eternal
barrier? . . . Madame Beck – Pere Silas – you should not
have suggested these questions. They were at once the
deepest puzzle, the strongest obstruction, and the keenest
stimulus, I had ever felt' (p. 491). Lucy's passion for
Monsieur Paul eventually overrides her fear of conflict,
masked as reticence, thus pushing her forward. A hypnotic
relation to reality, in which Lucy is motivated as if despite
herself, is finally broken. This gives her courage to explore
her experience, to give up defences, and so to change.

However before Lucy can win Monsieur Paul for herself
two things have to happen. She has to withdraw her projec-
tions, especially on to Madame Beck, and she has to stop
realising her desires negatively, most perniciously by regis-
tering an external defeat as an inner triumph. Moreover,
before reclaiming the power she has invested in Madame
Beck, Lucy has to recognise the headmistress as personi-
fying her own conscience:

> Two minutes I stood over Madame, feeling that the whole
> woman was in my power, because in some moods, such as the
> present – in some stimulated states of perception, like that of
> this instant – her habitual disguise, her mask and her domino,
> were to me a mere network reticulated with holes; and I saw
> underneath a being heartless, self-indulgent and ignoble.
> (p. 544)

A harshness which was previously directed on to herself is
turned back on its model. At once Lucy realises the school
itself is permeable, as smooth of exit as of entry. The narrative jumps into the present, creating an immediacy and
arousal lacking from the past tense leading up to it. Pressed
by a need for movement – heightened by a sleeping draught
given by Madame Beck – Lucy passes into the night:

> I wonder as I cross the threshold and step on the paved street,
> wonder at the strange ease with which this prison has been
> forced. It seems as if I had been pioneered invisibly, as if some
> dissolving force had gone before me; for myself, I have scarce
> made an effort. (p. 548)

This strange syntax – 'it seems as if I had been pioneered invisibly' – reflects Lucy's excitement; as she tours the streets of Villette, her curiosity – as marked as the fear which the same streets once provoked – is vivid. Yet something diverts her, keeping her from her destination: 'I knew my route, yet it seemed as if I was hindered from pursuing it direct: now a sight, now a sound, called me aside, luring me down this alley and down that' (pp. 551–2).

One last thing has to fall into place before Lucy can make her way forward. After eavesdropping at the night-long fête, a final revelation awaits her. On returning to the dormitory, Lucy finds a nun's habit flung on a bed – with this the spell is broken.

> Tempered by late incidents, my nerves disdained hysteria . . . In a moment, without exclamation, I had rushed on the haunted couch; nothing leapt out, or sprang, or stirred; all the movement was mine, so was all the life, the reality, the substance, the force; as my instinct felt. I tore her up – the incubus! I held her on high – the goblin! I shook her loose – the mystery! And down she fell – down all round me – down in shreds and fragments – and I trode upon her. (p. 569)

Lucy can only accept the nun as a mannequin once she has seen it, not as a nightmare vision, but as a revelation. By jumping on the mannequin she confirms the reality of a world independent from her, thus freeing her from her own imaginative extremes. From this moment a figment of her imagination can be laid aside as a fragment of reality, with none of its compulsive allure.

Free of her destructive fantasies and the defences they produce, Lucy still has to create a positive future for herself. This means accepting that a companionable relation to Monsieur Paul, for all its goodness, is at odds with the longing she feels for him. During the precious hours Lucy and Monsieur Paul spend together before he leaves for the Indies, a tightness creeps back into the narrative. Their happiness is oblique, nostalgic: 'once in their lives', the narrator tells us, 'some men and women go back to these first fresh great days of our great Sire and Mother – taste that grand morning's dew, bask in its sunrise' (pp. 591–92). This, apparently, is what Lucy and Paul go back to; however their dawn is brief, ending in the final pages with a stormy sea that gives with one hand and takes with the other. For all her efforts to transcend conflict, Lucy remains vulnerable to the 'great deep' within her. And so Brontë's story comes a full circle, closing on an ambiguous note. As long as Lucy remains loyal to a harsh maternal conscience, figured by Madame Beck, this circle will never break. The final pages may be meant to show Lucy embracing a solitary life, but they read like dry bread. Like Eugenie Grandet, Lucy can only love a man who isn't there, never to return; Monsieur Paul has to disappear at sea in order for Lucy to enjoy an enduring intimacy – beyond mortality – with him.

Lucy Snowe, a girl with a father so dead that he is never even mentioned, experiences the disappearance of love as an emotional death. This leads her to remove all traces of love from her life, and to banish her lover from it. Presumably because in this way she – and not fate – is the agent of her loss. Not surprisingly the hysterical structure remains very much in place at the end of *Villette*. It is significant that after ending the novel with Monsieur Paul drowning in the first edition, Charlotte changed the ending: at the urging of her father and friends she replaced it with an open ending that allows for a wishful reading. But despite this change the ending remained unequivocal for Brontë, who seemed to believe in a fatality at the heart of human relationships that went against happy endings.

While not all unrequited love is hysterical, certainly all hysterical love is unrequited; it can never be satisfied in reality, not least because it is not directed at a real person. No real experience of satisfaction can match a mythical one, any more than a contemporary lover can rival an archaic one. Having sought the goddess in her chamber, Lucy comes close to both handling her veil and daring her glance; yet the time Lucy spends with her is so fleeting, and so linked to imaginative extremes, that Lucy is soon alone again. The consequences for this novel are great: although *Villette* has the outward form of a *Bildungsroman*, a novel of an individual's formation, its fiery internal workings are closer to the wild tales Brontë wrote in her youth, where the role of reality is slight. However, if *Villette* proves nothing else, it is that an author who becomes hysterical because of what she can't quite remember, can still write well. Above all this is a novel that can't conclude: because Lucy never declares herself, never admits her passion for Monsieur Paul openly, her future necessarily remains open. By keeping her goddess secret and away from daylight, Lucy is spared the excitement – and risk – of bringing her into the world.

Notes

1. *The Brontës: Their Lives, Friendships and Correspondences in Four Volumes*, edited by Thomas J. Wise and John A. Symington (Oxford Head, 1933), vol. 1, p. 121.
2. Charlotte Brontë, *Villette*, edited by Mark Lilly (Penguin, 1953, 1981), p. 94. Further references to this text are given after quotations in the text.
3. *The Brontës: Their Lives, Friendships and Correspondences in Four Volumes*, edited by Thomas J. Wise and John A. Symington (Oxford Head, 1933), vol. 2, p. 115.
4. *The Brontës: Their Lives, Friendships and Correspondences in Four Volumes*, edited by Thomas J. Wise and John A. Symington (Oxford Head, 1933), vol. 4, p. 43.

4

Childhood, Boyhood – and Womanhood in Tolstoy's Early Novels

Hysteria has, classically, been seen as a female disorder. But the kinds of distress I have described as central to hysteria are experienced by men as well. The name for a certain kind of trouble may be gender specific – men are rarely *called* hysterical – but that doesn't mean that the malady respects such boundaries. This is a significant point with respect to hysteria because theorising about it has sometimes tended to see hysteria as revealing some essential frailty in women. Where a man might have been seen as undergoing an existential crisis, or as suffering a melancholy humour, a woman is more likely to be classed as hysterical – while living with approximately similar problems. If Proust, or Joyce, or D.H. Lawrence, or Andy Warhol had been

women what would we have said of their instability, hypochondria, hypersensitivity, and self-destructiveness?

But to take an example from the pre-Freudian era which
we are considering, it is clear from Tolstoy's early autobio-
graphical writings that he knew all about the hysterical
feelings he later illuminated in his highly-strung heroines. In
his early writings Tolstoy seems to be asking whether his
memory can be trusted, given his hankering for wayward
pleasures that distort it. Who is to say when memory stops
and fantasy starts in *Childhood, Boyhood, Youth*, Tolstoy's
story of growing up within an aristocratic family? This early
philosophical question, however, has a more desperate side
– when memory is experienced as unreliable, haunting and
deceptive. An inner tension, a ground of distress, opens up
which is not present – at least not at first – in intellectual
speculation about the reliability of memory as a source of
knowledge.

Unlike the tentative Lucy Snowe, Nicholas Irtenyev
relishes his role as narrator of *Childhood, Boyhood, Youth*; at
one moment proud of, the next embarrassed by, himself and
the family he lives gregariously among. As a narrator
Nicholas enjoys those moments when he becomes hysterical,
in contrast to Lucy who suffers hers. These episodes are
recounted as fascinating, as grounds for sympathy with and
interest in the young figure. When Nicholas opens his
father's desk and finds a locked portfolio that he knows he is
forbidden to open, yet feels he must, only to break the key in
the lock, the inevitability of his story draws the reader in.
This may be because Nicholas inhabits a world he experiences as fundamentally good, as safe and his by rights, and
this in turn encourages him to penetrate erotic secrets. In
contrast Lucy Snowe's world is less benign and so her sense
of risk is greater; for her a secret is as threatening as it is
exciting, and carries unthinkable dangers.

Childhood, Boyhood, Youth opens with the young narrator
Nicholas waking up and pretending to his German tutor that
he has just had a bad dream, about which he is so
convincing that he himself soon believes it. Already in this
scene the power of the imagination, a central theme of the
novel, is apparent. Nicholas is a striking narrator for his
directness and spontaneity: when his mother dies, shortly

into the story, he is terrified of the smell of her laid-out body, launching into a lengthy fantasy. Nicholas recalls his childhood on a prosperous feudal estate in tender and undefensive detail. *Childhood* explores the closed and secure world of a patriarchal estate, seen through a child's eyes. The easeful atmosphere changes abruptly in *Boyhood*, when Nicholas is told by his old friend Katya, 'you are rich, we are poor', thus confronting Nicholas with the reality of social differences. At this moment Nicholas realises how much bigger the world is than the family, friends, and acquaintances that have made his childhood so rich and entertaining.

As a spring storm floods the family carriage on their drive to Moscow, the narrative scope widens. A number of incidents follow, improvised in nature, only occasionally adding to what was explored in *Childhood*. Toward the end of *Boyhood* a young man who strives to self-perfection becomes Nicholas's friend, thus inspiring Nicholas to 'constant moral analysis'. Incident after incident is sparked by Nicholas's feelings of embarrassment, shyness, and shame; as if his feelings force him to accept the impact others have on him, despite his attempts to rise above them.

Childhood and *Boyhood* were written in the early 1850s; *Youth* was published in 1857 and is nearly as long as the early works together. *Youth* is a series of sketches about a young man's dreams of self-perfection, religious piety, sexual fancies, academic trials, moodiness, and social adventures. The significance of a young man becoming 'comme il faut' almost amounts to an essay. Tolstoy criticised *Youth*'s lack of unity and repetition, nonetheless its psychological analysis is often searching, particularly of the kind of emotional vanity that makes self-deception inevitable.

Tolstoy's trilogy is no golden tale of childhood. Nicholas's guile leads him to say everything; there is nothing and no-one he doesn't want to tell the reader about. The freshness with which he tells his story suggests that between his childhood and his later recall of it, his memory has remained intact. No matter how desperate his dealings with others become, he never loses confidence in himself, and so is never in danger of breaking down completely. Nicholas stays in imaginative contact with an early loved one, and this allows him to sustain the belief that he is loved. Even when he is unattractive and gauche in adolescence, and his father has the temerity to marry again, he never feels abandoned. He may lose an adored mother as a small child, but she never loses her place in his memory. Love for his mother, some of which becomes respect for his father, emboldens Nicholas in his experience of the world.

This is a benign form of hysteria: Nicholas is periodically taken over by intense feeling and is subject to massive projection and displacement which however doesn't involve a loss of self. The hysteria doesn't go *all the way down*; although it may flood Nicholas' personality at particular times, it doesn't usurp all his resources – although sometimes it seems to. The clear *Bildungsroman* format (looking back from the point of maturity to the troubled path by which it was arrived at) allows a joyousness to enter Nicholas' experiences which could seem horrible, if we didn't think that he was growing through and learning from them.

Caught between parents of opposing attractions – an absent, idealised mother and an affectionate yet neglectful father – Nicholas is spellbound by them. This is why his story never rests; something within it remains alive, never reaching climax or conclusion. It reappears in *Family Happiness*, a novella about the courtship of a naïve young girl and a middle-aged sceptic as recounted through the girl's eyes – as she looks back, now a married woman. The story is told through a woman's eyes – something Tolstoy never repeated. It is a story is about a couple who seek goodness, love, and sincerity through marriage; a man and woman who, in coming to despair of each other, also become disillusioned of these values. Their shared disillusion makes the novella melancholy in a way the earlier trilogy – which cuts off but doesn't end – never is, suggesting that Tolstoy doesn't know how to end a mature love story without being melancholy.

In his recreation of boyhood Nicholas Irtenyev goes to great lengths to describe his romantic adventures. One evening, trying to impress a girl at a party, he spoils a mazurka:

> I stopped short, intending to make the same kind of figure the
> young man in the first couple had executed so beautifully, but

just at the moment when I separated my feet and was preparing to spring, the princess, circling quickly round me, looked at my legs with an expression of blank inquiry and amazement. This look undid me. I got so confused that instead of dancing I stamped my feet up and down on one spot in the strangest manner, neither in time to the music nor in relation to anything else, and at last came to a dead standstill. Everybody was staring at me: some in surprise, some with curiosity, some derisively, others with sympathy.[1]

Nicholas is hysterical in the everyday sense of being carried off in a frenzy, but also in the deeper sense of offering himself up to the princess's scorn in a way that exaggerates his inadequacy. These antics seem only to multiply. When his first love, Sonya, rebuffs him, he becomes so pained that he is forced to appeal to the experience of an older man to describe his response: 'I was in the excited state of mind of a man who, having lost at cards more than he has in his pocket, is afraid to cast up his accounts and continues to stake desperately – not because he hopes to recover his losses but in order not to give himself time to stop and consider' (CBY p. 141). Even with hindsight, Nicholas doesn't want to count up what he has lost; he would rather keep on playing for girls than to think about how they may feel about him.

Far from suffering from reminiscences, Nicholas Irtenyev revels in his memories. This is a narrator who seems to understand the nature of memory, yet still can't help wishing it were otherwise. It is as if Nicholas knows that every memory is a creation of the present and to be enjoyed as this, and that to push beyond memory – to a time before it or to an experience outside it – is futile. There are however moments when Nicholas tries to revive an experience that inspires a memory, particularly when it involves his mother. He may accept that his mother is dead and can't be recovered, but it isn't an easy lesson; occasionally the idea that he can only bring back the past through memory becomes unbearable. At these moments, strongly hysterical, it seems he can't stand the knowledge that the only past he can have is the one he imagines for himself.

Like Levin in *Anna Karenina*, Nicholas struggles with the idea that he lives in a world without a guiding metaphysic. In so far as his world is meaningful it is due to the meaning he gives it, without transcendent help. This is something that Tolstoy's characters don't accept easily; many of them – especially those inclined to hysteria – would prefer that the meaning of their existence weren't dependent on themselves. Tolstoy is suggesting that ultimately we are all orphans, hence our shared fight for a place in the world. Success in this world, according to Tolstoy, is measured less by material gain than by an individual's capacity to move from family to wider society – and hence into his or her own authority. Central to this shift is the ability to interpret one's experience; to be a meaning-maker, a novelist, of sorts.

There is then no biographical version of Tolstoy's early years of which *Childhood, Boyhood, Youth* is a fictional reworking, since it is only in the act of creating Nicholas' childhood that Tolstoy gives imaginative reality to his own. (Nothing is real, Virginia Woolf once said, until it has been described.) Although Tolstoy was to become an accomplished author, creative writing didn't come easily to him, his imagination and memory never becoming smooth partners. The following scene recalls an afternoon when Nicholas sat daydreaming while his mother played the piano:

> Mamma was playing the second concerto of Field, her music-master. I sat day-dreaming, and airy luminous transparent recollections appeared in my imagination. She started playing Beethoven's *Sonate pathétique* and my memories become sad, oppressive, and gloomy. Mamma often played those two pieces and so I well remember the feelings they aroused in me. They resembled memories – but memories of what? It almost seemed as if I were remembering something that had never been. (CBY p. 40)

A rush of obscure feelings fill Nicholas, as if Beethoven has captured something he himself can't articulate. Music – Tolstoy's 'memory of the emotions' – sounds inner chords for which no words arise. Years later when his sister plays the same piece in *Youth*, Nicholas is still affected by it, but this time with nausea: 'I went into raptures when Lyuba played the *Sonate pathétique* though, if the truth be told, I had long been heartily sick of it' (CBY p. 266). Normally acute, there are moments, like this one, when Nicholas becomes irritable, insensitive, and lacking in insight – that is, quietly hysterical.

Time and again the young Nicholas shows how the past, filtered through his imagination, deceives: as soon as he recalls an incident, it alters. Anything worth remembering – especially his parents – comes back to him touched up. While both parents appear larger than life, a contrast between them is striking, with the soft cameo of his mother contrasting with the rollicking figure of his father. Nicholas' mother is a sensual ideal, which is perhaps why her son can never be in her company enough:

> She puts her other hand round the back of my head and her slender fingers run over my neck, tickling me. It is quiet and half dark in the room; I feel all quivery with being tickled and roused from sleep; mamma is sitting close beside me; she touches me; I am aware of her scent and her voice. (CBY p. 53)

His father is more unpredictable: he encourages Nicholas to eavesdrop on him at compromising moments, to identify with him in his fancies for women, and to regard him with admiring fear. This leads Nicholas to observe his father with an attentiveness that is missing from the airy visions of his mother:

> He was a man of the last century and possessed that indefinable chivalry of character and spirit of enterprise, the self-confidence, amiability and sensuality which were common to the youth of that period. He regarded the young people of our day with a contempt arising partly from an innate pride and partly from a secret feeling of vexation that he could not in our time enjoy either the influence or the success he had in his own. The two chief passions of his life were cards and women: he had won several million roubles in the course of his life and had had affairs with innumerable women of all classes. (CBY p. 38)

There are no prizes for guessing which parent Nicholas finds the most consoling to be near, and which he finds the most fascinating to be around.

This is a mother whose absence ennobles – 'the sound of her voice is so sweet, so warm. Just the sound of it goes to my heart!'. Not so Nicholas' father, who is kind yet teasing of his son's affections. In the middle of dealing with a long-suffering steward, his father pushes Nicholas from his desk: 'I did not understand whether this was a caress or a rebuke', recalls Nicholas, 'but at all events I kissed the large muscular hand that lay on my shoulder' (CBY p. 21). It is no wonder that two such different parents should promote hysteria in their son. The more his father philanders, the more Nicholas is pushed to take his father's empty place beside his mother – thus checking an identification with his father that would qualify his devotion to his mother. In failing to reconcile the purity of his mother with the worldliness of his father, Nicholas grows up to distrust both sexes, neither wanting to be like the led-astray man nor the ethereal woman. For the youthful Nicholas, a man's world – captured in the phrase *comme il faut* – is at once compelling and yet, ultimately, fatuous:

> I considered *comme il faut* not merely an important plus, an admirable quality, a perfection I was anxious to achieve, but an indispensable condition of life without which there could be no happiness, no glory, nor anything good in the world . . . The greatest evil this idea wrought in me lay in my conviction that the *comme il faut* was a self-sufficient status in society . . . that, having attained this state, he was already fulfilling his destiny and was even superior to the majority of mankind. (CBY p. 270)

This quality – fleeting yet essential – haunts the young Nicholas, who can neither assume nor reject it as an ideal. Especially when this manly pride, this fullness of self, turns out to be closely related to feminine vanity. In a diary entry of the period, Tolstoy describes vanity as 'a sort of self-love transferred to the opinions of others – a vain man loves himself not as he is but as he appears to others to be'.[2] This definition, in which the vain man is like the hysterical woman, explains why neither masculine nor feminine positions are open to Nicholas – since each conceals its treacheries, its false hopes.

Toward the end of *Youth* is a scene that reappears in *Family Happiness* – the novella which followed the trilogy – in which Nicholas experiences joy, melancholy, and tenderness inspired by a familiar concerto. Except that this time, because his sister and not his mother is at the piano, he can't enjoy it:

> I have never seen such a family likeness as there was between my sister and my mother . . . Lyuba smoothed the folds of her dress in exactly the same manner, turned the pages from the top with her left hand as mamma had, and pounded the keys

with her fist when she was vexed at not being able to master a difficult passage and cried, 'Oh dear!' and there was the same inimitable delicacy and precision in her playing of the beautiful piece of Field's. (CBY p. 164)

At the end of 'mamma's piece', Nicholas watches as his father takes his sister's 'head in his two hands and began kissing her on the forehead and eyes with such tenderness as I have never seen in him before' (CBY p. 165). It isn't clear whose side Nicholas is on at this moment – that of his sister's musical success, or his father's show of affection. His response is not simple jealousy: he is torn between identifying with his father's attraction to Lyuba's beauty, and recoiling – in loyalty to his mother – from it. This confusion is heightened when, minutes later, he overhears his father in the corridor, flattering a housemaid on her looks. The reappearance of piano-playing scenes in *Family Happiness* suggests that Tolstoy found it hard to accept the complex sexual feelings they evoked, and so was driven to repeat these memories in his next novel.

Before Nicholas can end his reflections on childhood, he has to answer a simple yet important question which applies to every individual entering adulthood. How can he release himself from his family without expelling himself from them entirely, nor pledging himself to them for life? Specifically, how can he appreciate the excitement his father offers, while remaining faithful to his mother's memory? How can Nicholas stop being the hysterical son of an adored and adoring mother, to become the outgoing son of a spirited father? Or will he always be torn between a love that is benign, generous, and selfless and one that is ambitious, pressing, and self-interested?

In his *Recollections*, written in old age, Tolstoy claims that an unselfconscious link with others, deep enough to be invisible, is the highest form of love. 'The love of others', he wrote, 'is a natural state of the soul, or rather a natural relation to people, and when that state exists one does not notice it'[3]. This is a far cry from Nicholas' youthful lust for the housemaid Masha, which is anything but invisible: she 'was very pretty but I am afraid to describe her lest my imagination should again present to me the bewitching and delusive image which filled my mind at the time of my infatuation' (CBY p. 123). Whereas a natural love of others is so taken for granted that there is no memory of it – there being no one moment when it is realised – sexual love is concrete, vivid, and detailed. Significantly when Nicholas' father – a passionate lover – remarries a woman Nicholas considers second best to his own mother, *Youth* breaks off. Unimpressed by this new mother, Nicholas is forced to find his inspiration elsewhere. However, although this means going beyond the family sphere and into the world, it needn't mean breaking his ties with family.

In his recreation of childhood Tolstoy shows a boy over-coming his hysterical tendencies; but never entirely, which is perhaps why they reappear, this time in a young woman, in *Family Happiness* – a novella published four years after the trilogy. In this novella the embarrassment of a hysterical hero is solved, at least superficially, by a heroine telling the story. *Family Happiness* (also called *Domestic Happiness* and *Happily Ever After*) is the story of an impossible demand made on love under the guise of marriage. Unlike Nicholas Irtenyev, who is looking for a perfect partner to end his romantic search, Sergei Mihailych is looking for a perfect relationship, for a woman who will share his values unre-servedly. Sergei would rather put the sharing of his values before the satisfaction of his wishes – a priority which turns out to be eminently hysterical.

Sergei's courtship of the young heroine Masha is equiv-ocal from the start. He seeks to persuade her of the vanity of youthful wishes and to win her over to an inhibited vision of marital love. Their courtship is a quiet struggle between civi-lised values and unruly passions: between Sergei's search for an enduring good and Masha's desire for the immediate and enticing. The outcome is predictable; Sergei's warning that society is just a bauble pushes Masha to pursue society even more, threatening their love in her search. The novella's epigraph from Michelet is apt – 'Il faut que tu crée ta femme' (you must create your own wife). And yet, beneath Sergei's desire to mould a girlish Masha into a suit-able wife, lies a hope for himself, which is that marriage will discipline his will.

Masha has her own reasons for seeking marriage. She too is in search of a frame through which to view and regulate her experience. But unlike Sergei, whose seniority suggests he has already enjoyed what the world has to offer, Masha can only speculate about life. As often happens in courtship, these two are drawn to each other in the hope that their difficulties will be resolved by being shared; rather than, as usually follows, compounded. Neither of them are comfortable with the excitement that their being together generates. Unsettled by her erotic feelings for Sergei, Masha has hopes of purifying herself of them:

> I was frightened at my own feelings – heaven knows to what length they might lead me. I remembered his embarrassment and mine when I jumped down to him in the orchard, and my heart grew very heavy. Tears streamed down my cheeks and I began to pray. And a strange idea came to me, reassuring me and bringing hope: I resolved to begin fasting that very day and prepare myself for Communion on my birthday, and on that day to become his betrothed.[4]

What Masha lacks within, she seeks outside, in this case through religious fervour. It is as if courtship is being used, by both Masha and Sergei, as a foil to their increasingly hysterical relations.

Publication of this novella upset Tolstoy deeply, undermining his position as an author. Writing shrilly to his publisher, he asks:

> What have I done with my *Family Happiness*! Only here and now, having come to my senses at leisure and having read the proofs you sent me of the second part, have I come to see what disgraceful s . . . this loathsome work is – a blemish on me, not only as author, but as a man.[5]

It is hard to reconcile this outburst with the unassuming novella of 1859, summarised by one critic as 'an unexciting story of courtship, early marital bliss, subsequent marital problems and eventual compromises, all from a young woman's point of view and in the prim conventionally proper, but perceptive style of a Victorian "lady-writer"'.[6] This charming story yet met with its author's wrath for being nothing but 'shameful, disgusting filth, and a moral and artistic botch'. Clearly something lies pressed within *Family Happiness* to have disturbed Tolstoy so much: this element is hysterical, and seems to arise from Tolstoy's own feelings, as a wary bachelor, of his own approaching marriage.

In keeping with Florence Nightingale's wry observation that nearly every romantic heroine has 'no family ties' and 'almost invariably no mother', Masha has lost both parents before the story opens. Grief for Masha's mother steeps the snowed-in house – a metaphor for the daughter's soul. Living aimlessly on an estate beset by financial troubles, Masha is on the lookout for something – or someone – to launch her story. Her grief is touched by regret for her passing youth; besides a morbid impulse 'to peep into that cold empty room' of her mother's, she suffers 'that helpless dreariness, from which by myself I had neither the strength nor even the will to escape'. But with the first signs of spring the family's ward Sergei Mihailych returns after a six-year absence and, as Masha notes, within 'five minutes he had ceased to be a guest and to all of us had become a member of the family'.

Even though a gap of nineteen years sets the youth and beauty of Masha against the moody middle age of Sergei, Masha is irresistibly drawn to him. Above all he reminds her of her father – 'his stories made me see my father as a simple, lovable person, whom I had never known till then'. From the start Masha's interest in Sergei is linked to an imaginary vision of her father. Sergei too is quick to establish Masha's likeness to her father: 'It's not for nothing you're so like your father. There's *something* in you. . .'. There is an intensity to this interest; Masha notes that 'his eyes had a special way of looking at one, direct to begin with and then more and more intent and rather sad'. This sadness doesn't stop him from trying to convince Masha to give up 'trivial' pleasures and to cultivate moral strengths in their place. The kind of selfless love Sergei would have Masha feel is captured in an eminently hysterical appeal Tolstoy made to a lover in a letter of this period: 'It's impossible to love for one's pleasure', he wrote her in a letter, 'rather one loves for the pleasure of another'.[7]

Having suspended his worldly desires, Sergei is content to keep the world at a distance: 'I could spend my whole life sitting here on this verandah', he comfortably admits to Masha. The love he finally offers her is paternal, since it involves holding an essential part of himself back. 'In spite of his constant effort to play down to me', Masha remembers,

'I was conscious that behind the part of him which I could understand there remained a whole other world into which he considered my inclusion unnecessary, and this did more than anything to foster my respect and attract me to him' (FH p. 24). This 'other world' attracts Masha, precisely because of her exclusion from it. Bound by the wish to please each other, they are soon joined by ties stronger than romance alone: as Masha remembers 'when he looked into my eyes and asked a question his very look would draw out of me the answer he wanted'. Surprised at this change, Masha realises that 'he was no longer the fond old uncle who spoiled or lectured me: here was my equal, a man who loved and was in awe of me as I loved and was in awe of him' (FH p. 32). A spontaneous reserve, the shadow of Masha's father, replaces their earlier shows of affection.

Masha proves her willingness to live up to high ideals by preparing for church communion, taking her away from Sergei for a time. Besides wisdom beyond her eighteen years, she gains a miraculous foresight:

> How I know, I cannot explain to this moment; but on that memorial day it seemed to me that I knew everything: whatever had been and whatever would be. It was like a blissful dream where all that happens seems to have happened already and to be quite familiar, and it will happen over again, and one knows that it will happen. (FH p. 43)

Masha's vision is elaborate yet vague and doesn't predict marriage. When, after a few days apart, Sergei does propose he has to overcome strong reluctance first. In conversation with Masha he discusses two scenarios with 'Monsieur A and Mademoiselle B', in the second of which Monsieur A 'grew to love Mademoiselle B as a daughter, and had no fear of loving her in any other way'. Not to be put off, Masha promptly offers a third possibility in which Monsieur A, having declared his love, discovers that Mademoiselle B returns it – as then happens between them.

Significantly it is only after Masha has pushed Sergei to propose that she allows herself to doubt their love: persisting in asking why he loves her, he replies, 'I don't know, but I love you', all the while staring at her 'with his intent magnetic gaze'. Years later Masha remembers the impact of this look:

> I made no reply, and involuntarily looked into his eyes. Suddenly a strange thing happened to me: first I ceased to see what was around me; then his face disappeared, until only his eyes seemed to be shining immediately in front of mine; next I felt that the eyes were inside me, everything became blurred, I could see nothing and was forced to shut my eyes in order to tear myself free from the sensation of rapture and awe which that gaze of his was producing in me . . . (FH p. 51)

Her dizziness hints at a pleasure first enjoyed with an early loved one; a pleasure which, escaping consciousness, leaves no memory. Sergei's penetrating look and the final ellipsis is a measure of Masha's devotion to her father, with her 'rapture and awe' indicating her unconsciousness of this link.

This romance seems meant to be – but by whom? During an annual memorial service for Masha's father, Sergei turns to Masha and remembers her father saying to him 'jokingly', 'you should marry my Masha'. Following their marriage service – as it happens – the next day, Sergei tells Masha she is entirely his, while she, for her part, recalls how his 'serene, happy eyes that held me captive rested on me'. In a carriage outside the church, Masha feels let down that she has experienced nothing more divine than hot flushes during the ceremony. Reaching out for Sergei, she remembers how 'I began to feel hot, my eyes sought his in the half-darkness, and all at once I knew that I was not afraid of him, that my fear was love – a new kind of love, tenderer and stronger than the old love. I felt that I was wholly his, and that I was happy in his power over me' (FH p. 55). In this sequence the daughter's desire for her father, which urges her – in fantasy – to give herself up to him, is a trigger for uncanny thoughts, looks, and gestures. In identifying with Masha's wish to marry her father, Tolstoy himself falls prey to its dizzying effects. This would explain why the service for the dead – yet evidently not dead enough – father is prelude to the daughter's marriage, and why Masha faints at the end of the scene.

Why should Tolstoy's identification with Masha be troubling, even shaming? Is it because a proposal from the father is something any young man should – out of self-interest – refuse? It would seem that in failing to admit the incest implicit in Sergei's desire to marry an old friend's daughter,

Tolstoy implicates himself in it. Rather than choosing a lover who removes her from her dead father's affections, Masha marries his stand-in. It was not only Tolstoy who overlooked this complexity; literary critics have also been blind to it. Aylmer Maude, Tolstoy's English translator, summed up *Family Happiness* as 'the most finished novel Tolstoy produced and the one which by its construction came nearest to an ordinary English novel' – giving no hint of the extraordinariness of this supremely 'ordinary' novel,[8] or the oddness of its climactic moments.

The second part of *Family Happiness* opens with a shift from Masha's to Sergei's family home. Masha finds herself in a house that 'went like clockwork' under the hand of her mother-in-law, while Sergei – hereafter 'my husband' – puts into practice his ideal of married life. Divided between his mother and wife, Sergei's loyalties are clearly stretched: 'every day without fail my husband would offer his arm to his mother, to take her in to dinner as he had always done, but she insisted that he should give me the other arm, so that every day without fail we stuck in the doorway and got in each other's way'. Despite this strain the couple do discover each other as husband and wife; but their discovery is short-lived. Within months Masha reflects, 'I began to feel lonely, feel that life was repeating itself, and that neither of us had anything new to give, and that we seemed to be forever turning in our old tracks'. Sadly, but not yet bitterly, Masha realises that marital harmony without the frisson of romance is not happiness at all: 'Loving was not enough for me after the happiness I had known in falling in love'. Gone is the joy of fulfilling her lover's desire as if it were her own; instead she swings, to her husband's alarm, from depression to 'transports of violent affection'. She begins to sense that every passing day 'riveted another link to the chain of habit which was binding our life into a fixed shape'.

Having exhausted her own romantic ideal, Masha's disappointment starts to show: 'my state of mind affected my health, and I began to suffer from nerves'. What was once enjoyed as romantic excess now finds expression, transferred to the nervous system, as hysteria. Once a forbidden pleasure – marriage to the father – has taken place, its zest seems to go. Without the canny knowingness which launched her in marriage, Masha becomes depressed. Anxiety takes the place of excitement and a lingering melancholy pervades the story. Instead of trying to find ways to express these changes, Masha starts suffering from nerves – as if this is the only channel open to her.

This is a story about a woman's struggle for her own terms of definition which would cast off those of others – making it a modern story. However this acquisition doesn't come easily, which is perhaps why Masha often talks about her marriage but rarely about herself. The implication is that her melancholy is caused by her marriage, as opposed to something within her. But is it? In a curious way Masha's and Sergei's marriage shields them from knowledge of each other; and, by extension, from themselves:

> When we were by ourselves – which we seldom were – I felt neither joy nor excitement nor embarrassment in his company: it seemed like being alone. I knew very well that this was my husband and not some stranger but a good man – my husband, whom I knew as well as I knew myself. I was certain that I knew everything he would do or say, and how he would look; and if anything he did surprised me I decided that he had done it by mistake. I expected nothing from him. In a word, he was my husband – and that was all. It seemed to me that this was as it should be, that it could never be and had never been otherwise. (FH p. 79)

Although the man Masha describes as 'my husband' has the same outward shape as the Sergei who proposed to her, now that his inner reserve has gone, and with it his mystery, he is unrecognisable to her. Instead of pleasure in each other's company, strained familiarity keeps them apart. Masha responds by not staying still for long enough to notice: 'I had no leisure for reflection and the regrets that these dimly-felt changes caused me I tried to forget in the distractions with which I was always surrounded'. But as the story shows, she never really forgets.

In keeping with the doctor who sends Kitty Shcherbatsky on a European holiday as a rest-cure in *Anna Karenina*, Sergei takes his wife to the lights of Petersburg. There she quickly revives: 'At the ball it seemed to me more than ever that I was the centre around which everything revolved, that it was only for my sake that the great ball-room was lighted up'. Shocked at her betrayal of their country life, Sergei feigns indifference to Masha's social triumphs. Masha doesn't care: she no longer wants to be loved singularly, self-lessly, and monogamously, but rather wantonly, selfishly, and thoughtlessly. Instead of deferring to her husband she starts lording it over him: 'I was so blinded by the sponta-neous affection which I apparently inspired from all around me, so dazed by the unfamiliar atmosphere of luxury and enjoyment; it was so agreeable to find myself in this new world not merely his equal but his superior'.

Caught in a social blaze Masha hardly notices time passing. Years slip by without event, apart from the birth of a son and the death of Sergei's mother – neither of which breaks the courteous veil the couple throw over themselves. Leaving her baby to her husband's care Masha visits a Euro-pean spa. There she is drawn to an Italian marquis who combines her husband's qualities, only more bewitchingly: 'young, handsome, elegant, and, above all, in his smile and the shape of his forehead he resembled my husband, but he was far better-looking'. Unlike her frozen marital relations, the marquis awakens in her a fiery passion: 'I did not acknowledge it to myself but I was afraid of this man, and against my will often thought of him'. And again, 'I hated, I feared him, he was utterly repugnant and alien to me; and yet at that moment the excitement and passion of this odious stranger raised a powerful echo in my own heart'. Despite her attraction, Masha is cautious, succumbing to remorse after a visit from Sergei. On board a train – a form of travel Tolstoy favoured for arousing reflection – Masha observes that 'a new light lay like a reproach on my conscience'. Cured of wayward desires, Masha is led back to a mature – but censorious – love.

Despite these stirrings of conscience, it is only with the coming of spring and a stay at her old home that Masha experiences lasting change. Familiar objects from childhood jolt her senses as her disillusion comes full circle – but this time without depression to mask it. Standing in her old bedroom where her children now sleep, she watches as,

suddenly from every corner, from the walls, from the curtains, old forgotten visions of youth crept out. Old voices began to sing the songs of my girlhood. What had become of those visions now, of those dear, sweet songs? All that I had hardly dared to hope for had materialised. My vague confused dreams had become a reality, and reality had become an oppressive, difficult joyless life. And yet everything here was just the same: the garden I saw from the window, the grass, the path, the very same bench over there at the edge of the dell, the same song of the nightingale by the pond, the same lilac in full flower, and the same moon above the house – and yet all so dreadfully, so desperately changed! (FH p. 88)

Unlike her passing regret after her affair, this disillusion has to be endured. There is nowhere for her to go – as Robert Frost put it, no way out but through. Alone in the house Masha sits down at the piano, having neglected its practice 'since the time of our first visit to Petersburg'. Facing an emptiness within, Masha struggles to imagine a future for herself:

But there seemed to be only a blank before me, I had no desires and no hopes, 'Can it be that my life is finished?' I pondered, and then, appalled, I raised my head and began to play the same andante through again, so as to forget and not to think. (FH p. 90)

At this moment her future looks empty because it is without hysterical love. Without this love, is Masha's life over? Tolstoy implies the opposite: it is only once Masha sits down to play the *Sonate pathétique* right through – alone – that she can overcome the urge for someone else to step in and create meaning for her.

Doubtless Tolstoy's response to publishing *Family Happiness* was dramatic, perhaps even traumatic, in the sense of being in excess of the event. By introducing a heroine who experiences the dizzying effects of wanting to be wanted – and in a sexual way – by her father, Tolstoy created a risky base for a pastoral romance. In so far as *Family Happiness* does end, it is to the strains of Beethoven's sonata, and on a note of maternal possession. To emphasise her new domestic power Masha takes her baby from her husband's arms, feeling as if 'none but I should look at him for long'. She then repeats 'Mine, mine, mine!' as she looks down at her baby, feeling a 'blissful tension in all my limbs'. This mother's child, a son, can now assume his place at the beginning of things, as sovereign to his mother. There is, it seems, no other beginning possible for a boy who will become the apple of his mother's eye.

Masha's recovery appears complete: she has learned to live and tell her tale, rather than suffering or experiencing it through others. And yet has she? Masha's attraction to Sergei may have lessened, but his command hasn't softened; and she is just as prey to longing, loss, and anxiety. Given that Masha married a man who is bent on squashing the qualities he initially found attractive in her – sensuousness and social charm – this is to be expected. Having chosen a man who resembles her father, Masha commits herself to a familiar, loved past, rather than an unknown future. It is as if she understands too few of her feelings to experience them as anything other than fate. So that when her husband's resemblance to her father becomes obvious she still doesn't see it. Instead she transfers her conflicts on to her husband – and, by extension, her children – and is seen, in the final paragraphs, living with the consequences.

In his passage from childhood to youth Nicholas Irtenyev gains a firm enough sense of reality to distinguish his imaginative – and occasionally hysterical – perceptions, from his perceptions of the world. This is never true for Masha, whose failure to recognise either her wishes or her depressions has the effect of distancing her from the world. *Family Happiness* circles round an unasked question that brought Tolstoy keen discomfort. Should he, as an author, identify with Masha's desire for her father, or with Sergei's desire for his friend's daughter? To do both, as in the dizzying carriage scene outside the church, or when the mother-in-law, son, and daughter-in-law get stuck in the doorway, makes the narrative jump and stumble. As if, by identifying with Masha's desire for her father, Tolstoy himself gets stuck in the doorway – through which his novella never quite emerges.

Notes

1. Leo Tolstoy, *Childhood, Boyhood, Youth*, translated by Rosemary Edmonds (Penguin, 1965) p. 80. Further quotations will be given in the text as CBY.
2. *Tolstoy's Diaries*, translated by R.F. Christian (Athlone, 1985) 20 March 1852, vol. 1, p. 44.

3. *The Works of Leo Tolstoy*, edited by Aylmer Maude (OUP, 1927) 'Recollections', vol. 21, p. 45–6.
4. Leo Tolstoy, *The Death of Ivan Ilyich and Other Stories*, translated by Rosemary Edmonds, (Penguin, 1960), p. 39.
5. *Tolstoy's Letters 1828–79*, edited by R.F. Christian (Athlone, 1978) vol. 1, p. 127.
6. *A Handbook of Russian Literature*, edited by Victor Terras, (Yale, 1985) p. 354.
7. *Tolstoy's Letters 1828–79*, edited by R.F. Christian, 9 November 1856, vol. 1, p. 74.
8. *The Works of Tolstoy*, edited by Aylmer Maude, (OUP, 1927) vol. 1, p. 415.

5

Seeking Help: George Eliot's *Daniel Deronda*

When a woman becomes troubled she needs the close interest of another in order to discover its meaning. Ultimately it is the interest – the curiosity – of another which allows her to grasp her own complexity. The intimacy that this kind of interest generates is especially powerful, bringing with it bad as well as good effects. It is this situation which George Eliot explores in her most ambitious novel, *Daniel Deronda*, published in 1876, five years after *Middlemarch*. F.R. Leavis believed that *Daniel Deronda* should be split into two and the best of it, the story of Gwendolen Harleth, published as a separate novel. However the stories of Gwendolen – mercurial, charming (and eventually desperate) – and Deronda – ambitious, serious, and questing – are not easily divided: the society marriage and anguished emotions of Gwendolen is keenly bound up with Deronda's dawning awareness – having being brought up an English aristocrat – of his Jewish ancestry. Much of the dynamism of the story comes from Deronda's relations with two women, Gwendolen and Mirah, who come to see him as a unique source of help in their troubled lives.

In the opening scene Deronda finds Gwendolen gambling in a European casino; driven to it, it transpires, in the hope of saving her mother and sisters from financial ruin. Only much later is it revealed that she is also in flight from an offer of marriage from Grandcourt – the great man of the neighbourhood – who, known to Gwendolen, already has three children with a woman who expects to become his wife. When, on returning to England, Gwendolen has to choose between a grand society marriage and a demoralising post as a governess, she decides, after some turmoil, to accept Grandcourt's offer of marriage.

Accustomed to exerting her will over others Gwendolen is taken aback at her husband's power over her, and she turns to Deronda for assistance. Although Deronda is sympathetic he never returns the intensity of Gwendolen's appeal; his interest is taken by Mirah, a lovely Jewess whom he saves from despair, and also by her brother, a Jewish scholar and consumptive. Deronda's recognition, after an interview with his fatally ill mother, that he too is Jewish, binds him to Mirah and Ezra so that their fates become synonymous with his own.

Gwendolen and Grandcourt go on a miserable yachting holiday in the Mediterranean, during which Gwendolen suffers her husband's cruelty. In Genoa, while sailing in the harbour, Grandcourt drowns before her eyes; when Gwendolen sees Deronda – conveniently on hand – shortly after the incident, she cries 'I saw my wish outside me'. Deronda is finally taken into Gwendolen's confidence, with an intensity that leads to Gwendolen's devastation when she discovers Deronda is to marry Mirah and depart for the East; as a result, the only hope she feels is left to her is to become the kind of woman Deronda had believed her capable of being.

During the novel Gwendolen changes from a wilful self-loving girl, to a subdued wife in the grip of a selfish husband, to a chastened widow with no definite future. Her tragedy is a steady downward spiral, with the narrator little concealing the murderousness that Grandcourt inspires in her. An important theme in the novel is creativity, with Gwendolen's brief forays into singing being contrasted to the dedication and artistry shown by other characters. The other

troubled heroine in this novel, the woman Deronda saves
from drowning and eventually marries, is Mirah. Mirah's
artistic aspirations are clear from the start, as are Gwendolen's; however Mirah uses her gifts whereas Gwendolen is
driven – out of anxiety – to trade in hers. Their situations
mirror each other: Mirah is humble where Gwendolen is
over-confident, Mirah is devoted to the difficulties of art and
becomes a great singer of Lieder – while Gwendolen cares
only for applause, an attitude which ensures that she will
never deserve acclaim. Hence Gwendolen's urgent desire to
sing seems all the more shallow because of Mirah's deeper
acceptance of her profession as a singer – itself a sacrifice of
wider ambitions.

Daniel Deronda keeps returning to the image of a young
woman with her arms outstretched, pleading: an image of a
woman who, beyond help, yet seeks it. This is the challenge
Deronda meets in Gwendolen; a woman who seeks to save
herself by pulling him into her despair. When Gwendolen
seeks help from Deronda, she experiences his help as
dependency, reminiscent of a child's relation to a parent.
The more Gwendolen attributes insight, integrity, and
autonomy to Deronda, the more she experiences a lack of
these qualities in herself. Like other troubled women, Gwendolen's appeal to Deronda triggers a loss of confidence in
herself. As Gwendolen's respect for Deronda grows, her own
confidence wanes; with the result that whenever he is near,
she is that much more attractive, lively, and promising than,
alone, she feels herself to be.

The fact that Deronda is willing to be caught up in this
way says something important about him – precisely his
fascination for the helplessness he has so far suppressed in
himself. While this isn't the only reason he responds to
Gwendolen's appeal, it is telling. It is through Gwendolen's
loss of hope, her inability to save herself, that Deronda
becomes someone capable of saving her: the extremity of her
desires launches him in a therapeutic role. The fact that she
asks too much of him, more than can be expected of another
person, is plain; and yet something about him encourages
her to ask it of him – rather than herself. As a result they
relate hysterically to each other, directing demands greater
than love on to each other.

It becomes clear in this novel that a woman's troubles effect everyone who comes into contact with them. That these troubles take a feminine form is hardly accidental. As a young woman George Eliot struggled to leave behind a type of femininity she experienced as hindering and to replace it with a hopeful and creative one. The qualities appropriate to a woman remained a sensitive issue throughout her life – as reflected in her handling of female characters in *Daniel Deronda*. Family and friends may perceive Gwendolen as bright, beautiful, and talented but the narrator holds no such illusions; far from being blessed, the narrator assumes that 'poor Gwendolen had both too much and too little mental power to make herself exceptional'.[1] This is a heroine who is characterised by her vulnerability, as revealed in her growing intimacy with Deronda. Although she tries to appear attractive and feminine toward him, this is to counter the badness within that she feels their intimacy has uncovered.

Gwendolen is described as spoiled, which suggests an early neglect which is forever – hopelessly – being made up for. This may be why she chooses Deronda as an intimate, in the unspoken hope that he can reverse this damage. However her choice fails; rather than their closeness overcoming inner conflict it has the effect of increasing it. Apart from her beauty and sensitivity, the narrator stresses Gwendolen's ordinariness. Deronda, in contrast, is exceptional from the first, and to no-one more than Gwendolen for whom he is unique among men. From the opening scene it is Gwendolen's insecurity, and not her passion, that enlivens her relation to Deronda. Although Gwendolen is the heroine and Deronda the hero, she never really loves him; fear draws her to him, and keeps her loyal. He may be indispensable to her, but he is always a threat, and so kept at arm's length; hence as her appeal becomes more urgent, his ability to respond to it lessens.

Daniel Deronda is one of a stream of realist novels, written in the late nineteenth century, to emphasise the vicissitudes of close relationships. Tolstoy's *Anna Karenina*, Thomas Hardy's *Jude the Obscure*, Maupassant's *Pierre and Jean*, and Turgenev's *Fathers and Sons* are all studies in the good and bad effects two people can have on each other.

George Eliot was acutely alive to the impact of intimacy at the level of imagination and conscience; and especially the extent to which each person in a couple creates their partner out of their own feelings and ideas. In conversation with Gwendolen, Deronda confides his view of close relationships, when he says that 'generally in all deep affections [loved ones] are a mixture – half persons and half ideas – sentiments and affections flow in together'. Bewildered that she herself might be half person and half idea to him, Gwendolen replies, 'I wonder whether I understand that'. Gwendolen is yet to discover that there might be a distinction between everything she feels for Deronda, and Deronda himself. As the novel unfolds she realises the need for this distinction, to the point of accepting that his purpose in life is not to relieve her distress.

Although Gwendolen's meeting with Deronda at a European resort seems chance, emotionally they were meant to meet, even had to meet. Their destiny is to create, rather than a grand passion, an intimacy the depth of which neither anticipates. A powerful reading of *Daniel Deronda* is as a story about the conversations Gwendolen and Deronda are able to have with each other – and, by implication, those they aren't. Their initial conversations, tentative and anxious, circle around what they are and aren't able to say to each other. Fired by mutual interest, their exchanges soon extend to confidences that share thoughts and feelings which are – often until that moment – barely known to themselves. On the occasions Gwendolen bares her soul to Deronda, she confronts truths she would rather no-one – including herself – knew.

There is a tradition, extending from Oedipus, to Hamlet, to Faust, which suggests that deep inner searching is always dangerous. George Eliot's epigraph to this novel – 'Let thy chief terror be of thine own soul' – appeals to this tradition, hinting that each of us possesses hidden powers which need guarding against. Our soul, she suggests, is not a place of sweetness and light, but somewhere to approach – if at all – cautiously. Stories that appeal to this tradition tend neither to please nor console; rather than people's fates being decided by God, nature, or even other people, blame is heaped on the individual. While Oedipus, Hamlet, and Faust are still key literary figures, no-one in similar situations today would be encouraged to follow in their steps. The modern way, it seems, is to hold back from exploring unseen depths. The final lines of Eliot's epigraph explains why one might be dissuaded from examining one's soul: 'There amid the throng of hurrying desires/That trample o'er the dead to seize their spoil,/Lurks vengeance, footless, irresistible'. In this sense *Daniel Deronda* is an old-fashioned novel, since Eliot dares to explore the souls of her characters, despite 'the throng of hurrying desires' and the waiting arms of vengeance.

Gwendolen Harleth's question, around which the novel turns, is profoundly hysterical: 'Am I', she asks, 'as bad as I fear I am?' Gwendolen discovers that she is torn between a desire for satisfaction and – more enigmatic and difficult – a desire for punishment. It is not that she enjoys being punished, more that she relies on the expectation of punishment to organise her extreme imaginative experiences. Ultimately Gwendolen's mistake is to treat her fantasies as if they were real, to the point of treating her daydreams as if they were actions. This mistake is horribly revealed to her in the depredation she experiences in her marriage to Grandcourt – a marriage which she had entered (to restore her fortunes) on the vain assumption that her charm would allow her to bewitch and control her husband. But Grandcourt emerges as an image of an utterly hard and indifferent reality. Because of the fierce hatred Grandcourt inspires in Gwendolen, and her fear of what it may lead her to do, she shuns her imagination altogether. Like many women who are driven to hysterical extremes, Gwendolen dreads her own lawlessness more than she minds being imposed on by others. For fear of what lurks within, she would rather be dominated by – rather than independent of – others.

Gwendolen Harleth has a way of prompting people to speculation about her. 'What was the secret of form or expression which gave the dynamic quality of her glance?', is the narrator's first question in the opening paragraph. Already she confounds a simple description of character: Gwendolen's character has an 'iridescence' which arises from the 'the play of various, nay contrary tendencies', including a 'large discourse of imaginative fears'.

Gwendolen's contrariness is in contrast with Deronda who is described as steady, considerate of others, and intellectually bold. And yet in important ways Gwendolen and Deronda complement each other; their intimacy opens up aspects of themselves which, without the other's encouragement, would otherwise remain hidden. Moreover, they look to each other for a vitality that both feel they lack individually, yet would like the other to provide.

It is crucial to this story that when Gwendolen and Deronda first meet they become intimates, as opposed to lovers. This is because at this point in her life Gwendolen needs intimacy more than she needs love. Before she can love another she has to be able to trust them first, and this is exactly what she is unable to do. A powerful theme in *Daniel Deronda* is the idea that someone's ability to love is the reward of having overcome barriers to intimacy. Gwendolen's greatest barrier to intimacy, which prevents her loving Deronda, is her fear of being known by him. As long as she can't bear his knowing her dark fantasies, she can't allow herself either to love or be loved by him.

Gwendolen's anxiety about intimacy is paradoxical: she desires to be close to Deronda nearly as much as she fears it. There is a tragic aspect to their friendship, which is that because Gwendolen is intimidated by Deronda, she never allays her fear that he will discover the worst about her, and so reject her. She cares too much about him to be able to care for him. Deronda interests her, but he also panics her, which is why so many of her thoughts about him are projective – that is, thoughts she imagines he has about her. In her eyes he possesses insight, love, and patience precisely to the degree that she longs for these qualities in herself. Eventually their intimacy puts such pressure on her that she becomes aware of 'something like a new soul, which had better, but also worse, possibilities than her former poise of crude self-confidence' (p. 378).

This new awareness upsets her 'crude' self-confidence – namely her triumphs in archery, courtship, and singing. It is significant that she loses confidence in herself the same moment that Deronda returns her jewels. These jewels are a gift from her dead father and are rashly pawned by Gwendolen, in order to pursue her luckless gambling – the first of her attempts to make fantasy (the fantasy of her own good luck) triumph over reality (the failure of her family's investments, her amateurism). The jewels are promptly returned to her, wrapped in Deronda's crested handkerchief. It is Deronda's sensitiveness in this matter that persuades her to take him into her confidence – and, simultaneously, to lose faith in herself.

The role Deronda plays in Gwendolen's imagination quickly outweighs his role in her life, and hers in his – in itself a clear sign of their hysterical relations. The long periods when they don't meet are essential to their friendship, giving them pause for the reflection that the intensity of their conversations prevents. These private speculations, vivid and intricate, take up far more of the text than their actual snatched exchanges. A measure of how important Deronda becomes to Gwendolen is to note how many times – and for how long – he enters her thoughts, independent of the time they spend together. In this way Deronda comes into Gwendolen's every decision, ghosting her reflections. Her investment in him couldn't be higher: 'without the aid of sacred ceremony or costume, her feelings had turned this man, only a few years older than herself, into a priest' (p. 485).

Deronda's attraction to Gwendolen is just as ardent, except that he is drawn to her erotic charm rather than the divinity she ascribes to him. Toward the end of their relationship he asks himself, 'How could his feeling for Gwendolen ever be exactly like his feeling for other women . . . strangely her figure entered into the pictures of his present and future' (pp. 683–84). Whereas he is a figure of conscience for her, she is a figure of passion for him. What Gwendolen finds in Deronda is a strong sense of right and wrong, whereas what he discovers in her is a vivid eroticism. Through their intimacy these potentials surface, to unsettle their conscious selves. This leaves them both with a crucial decision, which is whether to make something of what has been revealed of themselves, or to defend against it. Each makes this decision differently; while Deronda comes to appreciate his questing after knowledge and history, she hesitates, her fear of being found out as ever greater than any potential for good that lies within her being.

Once Gwendolen starts treating Deronda as a priest she no longer sees him as an equal – and nor he her. This doesn't make her the weaker partner, but it does make their relationship therapeutic, and the link between them asymmetrical. Whereas Gwendolen trusts Deronda instantly, he, for his part, never trusts her. Gwendolen makes a specific – yet largely unwitting – appeal to him, which is for him to accept her unwanted thoughts and feelings before returning them in a form she can absorb. Deronda accepts her appeal, partly for his own reasons, and only much later refuses it. Unhappily for Gwendolen, Deronda withdraws before she has reclaimed the parts of herself that she had handed to him for safe-keeping – leaving her no better able to deal with them.

Any story of salvation – which is ultimately what *Daniel Deronda* is – begs the question of who saves whom. Deronda is introduced as a susceptible young man with a tendency to identify with the fates of – often feminine – others. Gwendolen, on the other hand, is introduced as a young woman whose outward independence is at odds with her fear of being alone. Most conspicuous is her behaviour toward the decorative screen which is painted with a girl's drowning face and outstretched arms. When she faints on unexpectedly sighting this screen, there is no explanation, either from her family and neighbours or from the narrator. Clearly this is a heroine who needs saving – both from her harsh 'new soul' and the punishment that arises from it. This tension finds a focus in Deronda, who inspires Gwendolen's desire to be punished and then saved. Her attitude toward him reflects these contrary wishes, which is why after Gwendolen looks to Deronda to discover what upsets her, she recoils from finding out. It seems that no-one – including herself – is to be trusted with her desires and fears.

Deronda is not entirely willing in his therapeutic role, his feelings for Gwendolen swinging from a desire to help her, to an impulse to abandon her. Only as their acquaintance deepens does he realise that, even if he wanted to, he can't both help and save her. The contrast is vivid between Deronda's slow awakening to Jewish heritage and Gwendolen's downward-spiralling fortunes, her 'sick dream' – a mirror of his upward quest. The nature of Deronda's

responsibility to Gwendolen is never clearly stated. Is he
right in advising her to suppress her fears, or would she be
better off exploring them? Deronda's handling of Gwendolen,
exemplified in his advice to 'turn your fear into a safeguard',
is inherently paternal. Deronda is not the only source of
paternal advice; when Mrs Meyrick (the novel's incarnation
of wise maternity) comforts Mirah – the other troubled
heroine in this novel – she reminds her that 'anxiety is good
for nothing if we can't turn it into a defence' (p. 713).
Anxiety, according to Mrs Meyrick, is cause for further
defences, rather than a spur to examining what lies behind
them. Deronda may speculate on Gwendolen's fears
privately, but he never asks her directly what they are about,
or urges her to expand on them. This has the effect of
keeping her in a position of needing help – from him, as it
turns out.

By not being encouraged to explore her anxieties, Gwendolen is driven to enact them. A girl in whom 'passion had
begun negatively', and who seeks out the roulette table 'not
because of passion but in search of it', is discouraged from
looking within. This 'Spoiled Child' – the title of the first large
section of the novel – is to remain the object of other people's
concern. Deronda, in contrast, seeks neither help nor
advice, even though the doubts surrounding his parentage
are grounds for seeking it. In Deronda's mind Gwendolen
evokes disturbing images and feelings which are best
subdued – for his own peace of mind as much as for hers.

Before long Gwendolen comes to share his disquiet –
'among the forces she had come to dread was something
within her that troubled satisfaction'. From a therapeutic
standpoint, as opposed to a paternal one, there is little
chance that Gwendolen's disturbance will cease until she
opens up and talks about it. Had Deronda used his conversations with Gwendolen as an opportunity to talk about her
fears, she might have articulated them more fully. By
managing to interest her in her troubles Deronda goes some
way toward this, but not all the way – seemingly out of his
own nervousness that she will make his own conflicts about
sexuality and identity surface, perhaps even multiply.

There is an underlying psychological question in this
novel: Does Gwendolen's distress trigger her hysterical

outbursts, or is it its consequence? Does her conflict come from an inherent mental weakness, or is it the result of long-standing defences? Deronda treats Gwendolen's conflict as a sign of mental weakness, and urges further defences to allay anxiety. This paternal approach assumes that psychological problems afflict the mentally weak, in contrast with a thera-peutic approach which assumes that those who experience enduring conflict will eventually become – rather than start out – mentally weak. Had Deronda related to Gwendolen therapeutically he might have considered the emotions behind her distress, and linked them to less stressful ones, all with an eye to expanding – and thus strengthening – her awareness. In this way he might have made her fear and conflict worthy of attention, interesting even, rather than bewildering or frightening.

When Gwendolen takes fright at seeing the painted screen of a drowning girl, neither her family nor friends wonder what she is screaming at, or relate it to the rest of her behaviour. To them she is a highly strung young woman, rather than someone experiencing an understandable crisis. Instead of being urged to say what fills her mind when she sees the screen, the episode is hushed up. Had she been pushed to talk about what she saw her disquiet may have increased, but it may also have put her in touch with ideas and fantasies vital to comprehending it. However no-one comes forward to suggest that if she can endure this crisis, and can find words to express it, she may well transcend it.

Gwendolen seems destined to struggle against herself; she lives in terror of what her imagination might inspire her to do and where her fantasies might lead her. The story is however well developed before we are told why she is anxious, excited, and fearful of herself. Gwendolen, it turns out, is frightened of wanting something that can only be hers at the expense of another woman's happiness – namely Grandcourt's hand in marriage. Although at the novel's opening Eliot cleverly withholds the reason for Gwendolen's trip to Europe, it turns out that she is running away from the knowledge of Grandcourt's first wife – pretending not to know what she already knows. The rich, but as it turns out, internally dead and deadening Grandcourt, figures in the story as a sort of Faustian salvation to Gwendolen.

Grandcourt's wealth and prestige are evident to all, but a devastating meeting with Mrs Glasher – who has borne Grandcourt four children and has now been unceremoniously shunned – reveals Grandcourt's hidden cruelty and infinite egotism. So the offer of Grandcourt's hand comes just when the stakes have reached their highest. At this point Gwendolen can see no other way of satisfying her need for distinction and grandeur, even though this requires her to isolate Mrs Glasher still further (by in effect disinheriting her and the children) and by pitting her seductive charm against Grandcourt's inhumanity, in the hope that she will be able to master this appallingly masterful man.

However by refusing to sympathise with Mrs Glasher's plight and determining to marry Grandcourt, Gwendolen makes it more likely that she too will be let down by love – just like Mrs Glasher and her own widowed mother, Mrs Davilow. From the moment Gwendolen meets Mrs Glasher, getting what she wants – wealth enough for herself and family – is aligned with getting what she deserves, which turns out to be a kind of moral whipping.

Gwendolen has a choice, either to encourage Grandcourt or to respect Mrs Glasher's claim. Apart from doubting Grandcourt's fidelity as a husband, she clearly doesn't love him – but she is excited by him. The way he draws her into parts of herself that she is otherwise shy and nervous of is masterly. In his company she becomes aware of her 'subjection to a possible self, a self not absolutely to be predicted about, [which] caused her some astonishment and terror'. This new unpredictable self upsets her to the extent that 'her favourite key of life – doing as she liked – seemed to fail her, and she could not foresee what at a given moment she might like to do' (p. 173). When Grandcourt does propose, instead of being excited, she is frightened by the imagined consequences: not so much that Mrs Glasher will retaliate, but that she – in identifying with a spurned wife – will invite the same fate.

Despite the problems that marriage brings Gwendolen, it also brings her distinct advantages. The vision of Mrs Glasher's haunting face, combined with her husband's contempt, together give Gwendolen something to organise her – previously unmanageable – fears around. The older woman's face becomes a focus for negative fantasies which gradually become conscious: 'Gwendolen, watching Mrs Glasher's face while she spoke felt a sort of terror: it was as if some ghastly vision had come to her in a dream and said "I am a woman's life"' (pp. 189–90). This face may be unwelcome but it is nonetheless company, which is significant for a young woman who hates to be alone. From now on this face comes into Gwendolen's mind whenever she needs to offset a sense of boundlessness within.

This heroine's greatest fear, it turns out, is her hatred of others. 'I shall never love anybody. I can't love people. I hate them', she tells her mother after rudely turning down an offer of marriage from a pleasant young neighbour who is genuinely in love with her, but whose portion and prospects are modest. Any sustained closeness is unbearable to Gwendolen, and soon broken off. It is a bitter irony that Grandcourt's undemonstrative nature initially makes him bearable to Gwendolen – she relies on the fact that he is always cool and unexcited, without pausing to enquire what he must be like inside to live at this pitch of cool contempt for others, a contempt which (given his wealth and social position) comes across as perfect good-breeding, a complete unflappability borne of a refusal of sympathy. It is no surprise, then, that Gwendolen is confused to hear Deronda say that 'affection is the broadest basis of good in life', and that he takes his interest in others for granted – 'call it attachment, interest, willingness to bear a great deal for the sake of being with them and saving them from injury'. Bemused, she replies, 'I wonder whether I understand that'; and then, 'I believe I am not very affectionate; perhaps you mean to tell me, that is the reason why I don't see much good in life' (p. 471). This is exactly how Grandcourt sees life, too; he represents the horror of what Gwendolen might be, and fears she will become, if she can't hold on to Deronda.

Gwendolen Harleth is a cautionary heroine who is prey to forces in the mind which can overwhelm positive feelings, in the grip of which hatred may destroy love. Whether she is responsible for this is unclear, however there is a clue in her being described as spoiled. Someone who is spoiled suffers doubly: initially from an experience of neglect and later from attempts to reverse it. Being spoiled makes Gwendolen intensely dependent on Deronda, since she comes to believe that only he can save her from wickedness – that is, from indifference. Whenever a crisis looms, in her imagination only Deronda can avert it. Toward the end of their relationship she reminds him that 'if you had not been good, I should have been more wicked than I am' (p. 767).

Gwendolen doesn't so much decide to marry Grandcourt as decide not to turn him down. After wakeful nights of bad dreams she determines 'to do as she would if she had started on horseback, and go on with spirit, whatever ideas might be running in her head'(p. 357). These ideas, cut off from meaning through her impatience and panic, are what Gwendolen appeals to Deronda to make sense of. When Deronda visits the Grandcourts, weeks after her marriage, he appears 'unique to her among men, because he had impressed her as being not her admirer but her superior: in some mysterious way he was becoming a part of her conscience' (p. 468). Having absorbed Deronda as a touchstone of right and wrong, she no longer needs his physical presence: now that she has taken him into herself, even the memory of his 'severe words' is enough to curb her desires.

Gwendolen is not the only character to experience passion negatively in this novel. It finds an echo in Princess Leonora Halm-Eberstein, Deronda's distant, ultimately found and just as soon lost mother, when she explains her failure to overcome her father's influence. 'I don't consent', she explains to Deronda, 'we only consent to what we love. I obey something tyrannic'. Rather than challenge her father and her Jewish ancestry openly, Leonora becomes an opera singer, internalises her suffering, and invites an early death. 'I wished I could have defied him openly', she tells Deronda, 'but I never could. It was what I could not imagine: I could not act it to myself that I should begin to defy my father openly and succeed' (p. 695). She goes on, 'I have been forced to obey my dead father. I have been forced to tell you that you are a Jew, and deliver to you what he commanded me to deliver' (p. 693). The rule of her dead father is more profound than that of her real father ever was: from a living father Leonora could run away, but from a dead one she can't escape. Forced to obey a force stronger than self-interest and love, Leonora sacrifices herself. Leonora's conscience is a hostile paternal presence; her dead father is an irascible, unloving parent whose legacy is a curse.

Gwendolen's story reaches a climax the morning she sees 'her wish outside her' in the form of her drowning husband. The day before Grandcourt drowns in the harbour at Genoa, and Gwendolen's wish comes true, she makes a final appeal to Deronda on the hotel stairs. She means to ask him if he can cut a new key for her dressing case which contains a small silver knife. But she loses courage, thinking she will arouse his suspicions, and doesn't ask. This knife, the focus of Gwendolen's murderous fantasies, is hidden from Deronda until too late. Nor can she bring herself to tell Deronda about the dream she had had that morning: 'a strangely-mixed dream in which she felt herself escaping over the Mont Cenis, and wondering to find it warmer even in the moonlight on the snow, till suddenly she met Deronda, who told her to go back' (p. 740). Neither direction is open to Gwendolen: behind her lies the drowning face and in front stands Deronda. Like Romola outside the gates of Florence, ordered to go back to her husband by Savanorola, Deronda is both Gwendolen's mentor and jailer – to the point that 'the strife within her seemed like her own effort to escape from herself' (p. 746).

When she sees Grandcourt in the water before her, with his arms outstretched, the spell of the drowning face breaks. Instead of the fantasied consequences of her wishes, Gwendolen now has real ones to confront. However it is not until Gwendolen makes her confession to Deronda that her murderous fantasies come to light. Central to these fears is the silver ornamental knife which, since early marriage, she has persisted in not using – except in fantasy. Like the image of Mrs Glasher's face, the willow-shaped knife has a dual function which is to provoke and then to organise Gwendolen's anxiety. Unable either to possess the knife fully, or to throw it away, it becomes the focus of her night-marish fantasies. Above all the silver knife is linked to the painted screen of the fleeing girl, in that both spur fantasies involving a woman in flight from something terrible. As a symbol, the knife also stands for what happens when a thought and a feeling are cut off from each other, leaving

only anxiety as a link. As long as Gwendolen is prey to
anxiety of this kind, no escape is open to her.

With Deronda's encouragement Gwendolen establishes a
number of symbols – the painted screen, Mrs Glasher's face,
the silver knife, his own 'severe' words – as a defence against
anxiety. He never suggests that her fears might be fuelled by
fantasies she doesn't dare share; instead he urges her to
experience her fears as a warning, and hence to suppress
them. Deronda fails to explain that this advice leads to a
psychological dead-end, that a suppression on this scale
depletes one's potential for positive feelings. By putting all
her energies into defending against intense excitement her
store of eroticism runs low, which in turn makes her prey to
her own destructiveness. All these consequences are with-
held from her, and so she continues her education in fear.

The willow-shaped knife stands for Gwendolen's desire
for revenge, for an excitement so extreme that it must
remain a fantasy. Convinced that should she hint at her
fantasies to Deronda he would reject her, Gwendolen – with
the narrator's help – conceals the truth. And since she goes
further in conversation with Deronda than even in her own
thoughts, she hides the truth from herself, too. It is ironic
that Gwendolen is inhibited less by her tyrannical husband
than by the person she believes will free her – Deronda.
'Take your fear as a safeguard', he presses her. 'It is like
quickness of hearing. It may make consequences passionately present to you' (p. 509). He urges her to imagine her
wishes realised, to feel the appropriate guilt, and to overlook
the rage which fuels them. By holding fast to Deronda's
example she is to rise, miraculously enough, above wickedness. Except that – in a direct reversal of Deronda's upward
path to enlightenment – Gwendolen's descent is slow and
sure. Having absorbed Deronda's influence – 'that severe-
browed angel' – as a brake against anxiety, she uses his
severity to keep the exciting and the unacceptable at the
edge of, but never quite out of, her awareness.

Once more Gwendolen has a choice, this time to accept
her wishes as meaningful or to fly from them. If she can
resist flying from them, while avoiding the impulse to lean
harder on Deronda, this is a moment of hope. By not
escaping in either direction, and in taking her wishes

seriously, she may not need saving from herself. The challenge to Deronda as he listens to Gwendolen's broken
confession, her stumbling reminiscence, is rather different.
What Gwendolen is asking of him as a witness to her confession is to find an acceptable story in it. In this Deronda
succeeds; he is able to treat what Gwendolen says as a
story, as a meaningful sequence of thoughts and events. As
a result she sees her fantasies as fantasies, and hence they
no longer move 'within her like ghosts'. But this respite is
short-lived, because as soon as she hears Deronda is to
leave England, perhaps for good, she – once more the spoiled
child – breaks down.

   There is however no going back, with or without
Deronda's support, now that Gwendolen's confession has
been heard. The question, rather, is whether her fantasies
will run to extremes, or whether she can stay with the
conflict which fuels them. In attempting to stay with her
conflict, Gwendolen suffers, mainly because she now knows
what upsets her. She was, the narrator says, 'undergoing a
sort of discipline for the refractory which, as little as possible
like conversion, bends half the self with a terrible strain, and
exasperates the unwillingness of the other half' (p. 656). As
if in sympathy with this strain, the narrative appears also in
shock, stopping and starting unexpectedly. Whereas in the
manuscript 'a great wave of shock passed through Gwendolen's soul', this is altered to 'a great wave of remembrance'
in the first edition (p. 876). Memory and understanding
seem finally to have gained the upper hand over Gwendolen's excitement and fear. A shock which Gwendolen can't
bear thinking about has become a series of memories –
which no longer causes her to faint.

   And yet has it? Is it shock or remembrance that shakes
this heroine at the end of a novel which ends, as it begins, in
medias res? What exactly has Gwendolen learned, except
that she is dominated by those she is closest to? Are we to
suppose that a spoilt girl, a young woman driven to negative
satisfaction, has undergone a change of such depth that her
former anxiety and 'lawlessness' within has been relieved by
recounting, just once, 'the terrible history of her tempta-
tions'? The fact that Gwendolen goes on to imagine her story
'through and through again' suggests that it is repetition,

and not understanding, which stamps her recall. Equally, would she feel anguish at hearing of Deronda's departure if she were free of his influence? Far from being liberated into a fuller sense of herself, Gwendolen appears just as bent on relieving anxiety in ways that delimit her: despite her withdrawal into family life in the country, she takes her inhibitions and tensions with her.

Rather than inspiring Gwendolen to grapple with mental conflict, with a view to surviving it, the advice of this novel is to defend against it. The most effective defence for women, according to this narrator, is the fear and awe inspired by an intimate – and invariably masculine – superior. Feminine susceptibility is to be encouraged, not tempered – even though a man who inspires fear and awe in a woman is more likely to fuel than to allay her anxiety. As the narrator observes, 'Deronda had lit up [Gwendolen's] attention with a sense of novelty: not by words only, but by imagined facts, his influence had entered into the current of that self-suspicion and self-blame which awakens a new consciousness' (p. 485). As soon as they meet, Deronda convinces Gwendolen that she needs to be on guard against her imagined wickedness. When Deronda sails for the East, just before the novel ends, Gwendolen is bewildered; after all, she 'could not spontaneously think of an end to that reliance, which had become to her imagination like the firmness of the earth, the only condition of her walking' (p. 867). This dependence is paradoxical, since she depends on him to defend against the fear and excitement which is – in part – an effect of their intimacy. Similar to other troubled women, Gwendolen's dependence on Deronda works against the development of her independent self.

Gwendolen's spiralling fortunes beg further questions. Does her wickedness reflect a fantasied evil or an actual wrong-doing? Is she to be punished for wishing her husband ill, or for doing him real harm? The morality Gwendolen is pushed to adopt is taken from Deronda: as the narrator observes, 'it is hard to say how much we could forgive ourselves if we were secure from judgement by an other whose opinion is the breathing medium of all our joy' (p. 833). Gwendolen is advised to sharpen her conscience by modelling it on the harshness of another; even though for Gwendolen to grow imaginatively stronger, she needs to free her thoughts and feelings and to discover resources of her own. This however is far from the novel's recommendation which is that Gwendolen should be punished for her fantasies – which is why *Daniel Deronda* is, despite its fascinations, a dark novel.

In failing to overcome her fear that Deronda will reject her, and in experiencing his departure as a rejection, Gwendolen collapses. Largely through Deronda's insistence that she banish bad thoughts from her mind, Gwendolen is in a considerably weaker state than at their first meeting in the casino. In advising her not to interest herself in fantasies of wickedness, except as a caution, Deronda also prevents her from exploring positive fantasies. This is mistaken: fantasising, loving, and thinking are closely related, and so a withdrawal in one area effects every other. When Gwendolen worries about taking her thoughts too far, she is also worrying about taking her affections too far. Consequently when she has thoughts about hating people, she is tempted to break off thinking altogether – especially when those she can't bear thinking hatefully about are the ones she otherwise loves.

Ultimately it is Deronda's faith in a world which respects his claims on it that saves him. In contrast, Gwendolen's anxiety about finding someone to love in a world with no obvious place for her, is what undermines her. Her dread of the future and her struggles with conscience find a dramatic counter in Deronda's hopeful sense of destiny – which leads him to seek out the very solitude, open spaces, and darkness that she is compelled to avoid. These characters transform themselves in opposite directions: Deronda in an open embrace of the world, Gwendolen in a shrinking away from the possibilities left to her. While in narrative terms Gwendolen marries Grandcourt and is drawn to Deronda, emotionally she enters into complex relationships with two men who stand for two sides of her conscience – the severe and the benign. Grandcourt stimulates her murderous desire for 'something my fingers longed for', the silver knife, while Deronda increases her yearning for a spiritual grace that is finally closed to her. Through their joint influence they reveal what it is that troubles satisfaction within her, but without ever helping her to overcome it.

Gwendolen's disquiet is the focus of various mirror scenes: in Europe when she looks lovingly at her reflection, and compares it with her family's lacklustre fortunes; after the impresario Klesmer points out her lack of musical talent – making her face, suddenly pale, look like another woman's; and when her stricken look is caught in the mirror above the fire, having unwrapped the diamonds sent by Mrs Glasher the very evening of her wedding. On all these occasions Gwendolen's beauty is contradictory. After all, what is her beauty worth if she experiences herself as stripped of value? Gwendolen's helplessness is, finally, a form of hopelessness; she has neither the power to attract a loving other, nor to engage their support. At certain moments, for example when she can't decide whether to embrace or distance Deronda in Genoa, this struggle overwhelms her. George Eliot's answer is that Gwendolen should accept this conflict, using the anxiety it arouses as a corrective. However this overlooks the emotional fact that by learning to live in the shadow of this conflict, Gwendolen is learning to live without the love that might release her from fantasies of being saved.

Notes

1. George Eliot, *Daniel Deronda*, edited by Barbara Hardy (Penguin, 1976) p. 667. Further page numbers are given in brackets in the text.

6

'An old woman at thirty': Florence Nightingale's *Cassandra*

A hundred and fifty years ago, a woman who felt weary of life at thirty could blame her weariness on being unmarried. If only, she and others around her believed, she could engage herself to the right man, she would not feel at odds with life. Florence Nightingale, having declined various marriage offers, was weary of life at thirty; moreover the heroine of her novel, *Cassandra*, dies at this age. Today it is hard to conceive of Florence Nightingale as other than famous, or to credit her suffering as an idealistic young woman. It is equally hard to imagine that when Florence was born in 1820, to well-to-do parents on a continental tour, the idea of calling a child after an Italian city was novel; yet by the middle of the century thousands of English girls were called Florence, and not for its associations with Italy. This national heroine's life is a paradox: while the whole of England was impressed by her, something stopped her being impressed by herself. Having become an influential woman, in her own eyes she was a failure. Given the zeal with which she set things to rights in the Crimea, and reformed the training of nurses on her return, why wasn't she satisfied with her achievements? Above all, why did she squash her novel *Cassandra* along with her romantic ambitions?

Many have passed Florence Nightingale off as a sexless do-gooder – Lytton Strachey satirised her as 'the saintly, self-sacrificing woman, the delicate maiden of high degree who threw aside the pleasures of a life of ease to succour the afflicted' – but this is mistaken. Rather what her example shows is how distinct a women's inner and outer life can be, especially when depression is involved. Florence Nightingale's inability to feel good about herself was at odds with her worldly triumphs and remained so throughout her life. Her push for public reform contrasts starkly with her private plea in *Cassandra*, written shortly before she left for the Crimea. Cassandra's voice, weary yet passionate, unmistakably depressive in tone, is proof that the only success worth having is the kind that is internal: a woman who cannot credit herself risks dying – imaginatively long before physically – of low spirits. Cassandra is this woman; true to the myth she dies young, unlike her author who soldiered on, nursing numerous ailments, well into old age. And yet what were Florence's advantages, attractiveness, intelligence, and indominability worth if she herself couldn't appreciate them?

As a young woman Florence Nightingale was depressed by aims she fell short of, and ideals she couldn't uphold. On reaching thirty she made a pact with herself; despite the world's indifference to her erotic and ambitious wishes, she would yet strive to fulfil them. Although with time she gave up her more extravagant wishes, she never gave them up entirely, and these haunted her through depression. Perhaps the strongest of these was the desire to save others. Whereas Gwendolen Harleth was driven by her desire to be saved, Florence – publicly at least – was driven by her desire to save. This masculine wish yet conceals feminine elements: while on the surface Florence wants to care for others so as to feel needed by them, deeper still – and hence suppressed – she wants to be wanted in a feminine and possibly erotic way by them.

During a trip to Greece on her thirtieth birthday, Florence wrote in her diary, 'I thought I would go up to the Eumenides Cave, and ask God there to explain to me what were these Eumenides which pursued me. I would not ask to be relieved of them – welcome, Eumenides – but to be delivered from doing further wrong. Orestes himself did not go on murdering'.[1] Florence is no longer trying to escape her furies; she is seeking them out, assuming they have something important to tell her. Lytton Strachey describes Florence as possessed by demons, however the idea of her being possessed by furies seems more apt.[2] Whereas demons are driven by sin, furies are avenging spirits in the service of a higher being. Florence was driven by furies; these were the spirits which pushed her on and, eventually, wore her down.

Florence Nightingale went through in an extreme form what she claimed most women undergo mildly. By identifying with Cassandra she showed her defiance of an unaccommodating world, her refusal to let it press down on her. And yet the act of writing about Cassandra saved Florence from becoming her, and so meeting the same fate. Instead she shook off her depression, faced her own furies, and made their energy her own. Determined not to count herself among those women who are 'practically dead long before they are physically dead', she directed her wishes away from fantasy and concentrated on realising them in the world. In the margin of Browning's *Paracelsus Aspires*, she wrote that 'pursuing an aim not to be found in life, is its true misery' – which suggests a lesson learnt the hard way. By giving up idealistic aims she released energy for worldly ones, and in this way empowered herself. Hence the decision to change the title of her voluminous account of the human condition from the brisk and metaphysical *A Short Account of God's Dealings With the Author*, to the pragmatic and accessible *Practical Deductions*. With this shift she became accountable to herself, in the absence – it seems – of anyone higher to be accountable to.

Essentially a cry in the dark, *Cassandra* marks Florence's break with feminine desires to be loved and saved, and her preference for the more masculine desire to be indispensable to others.[3] With age Florence turned the blame for her own frustration away from herself and on to the world – from now on it wasn't she who constantly fell short, but everyone else. Having got over the discouragements of her youth, Florence had little sympathy for her younger daydreaming self. Following her success in the Crimea, she transformed her home, and especially her bedroom, into a hive of political activity. With so much to do indoors she felt less and less incentive to go out. Her expression took on a certain fixity, the ribbons went from her dresses, and her society shrank to one visitor in her bedroom at a time. Rather than treating male visitors as suitors, she shunned marriage and used men for political ends.

The myth surrounding Florence's later life obscures the precariousness of her early years. Journals and letters of the period reflect a girl in a daily struggle with her own turmoil. In many ways Florence's youth echoes that of Theresa in George Eliot's *Middlemarch*:

> What were many-volumed romances of chivalry and the social conquests of a brilliant young girl to her? Her flame quickly burned up that light fuel; and, fed from within, soared after some illimitable satisfaction, some object that would never justify weariness, which would reconcile self-despair with the rapturous consciousness of life beyond self.[4]

Like Theresa, Florence desired a 'life beyond self'; she too sought 'some illimitable satisfaction' which might justify her efforts and make it worth subordinating her personal wishes to it. And yet unlike Theresa, Florence overcame this impulse. At a certain point she stopped wishing for what life couldn't deliver, appealed to the world as she found it, and demanded satisfaction from it.

This transformation was however gradual. The first thing to go was Florence's tendency to daydream; and what better way to rid herself of it than to write a novel in which the heroine dies from too much daydreaming? A heroine who, moved by her own furies, condemns both herself and the world. With her love of Greek literature, Florence knew that Cassandra had to die denouncing an indifferent world. One innovation was to get Cassandra's brother to tell Cassandra's story, recalling their final conversations after her death.

Although the pen and ink manuscript of *Cassandra* which is in the British Library has slashing cuts, it has recently been published alongside Florence's longer and more abstract *Questions for Thought*. The most radical change Florence made to the original manuscript, making it possible for her to publish it privately, was to suppress the first-person heroine and to replace it with a noncommittal 'we'. The story of a woman 'who has neither the courage to resist nor to submit to the civilisation of her time', in the manuscript, becomes the story of an anonymous 'one' in the published version. This unnamed Cassandra speaks on behalf of all women; while yet despairing of finding a woman whom she considers it worth identifying with. Moreover her resistance to her times is curiously empty; having rejected the world as it is, she is helpless to change it.

In order to change a novel about a doomed heroine into a social polemic about the constraints suffered by all women, Florence had to make bold cuts. First her heroine Nofriari – an Egyptian Cassandra – disappeared, to become an unnamed 'one'. Next to go was Nofriari's fantasy companion: 'I was accompanied by a phantom', she explains in the manuscript, 'the phantom of sympathy, warming me, guiding me, lighting the way for me. It was only an idea, it never reached, even in my own mind, reality'.[5] This very personal phantom, who promised so much yet delivered so little, becomes the companion of all women in the published version: 'women are accompanied by a phantom – the phantom of sympathy, warming, lighting the way' (*Cassandra*, p. 219). In the final version *every* woman is guilty of daydreaming and of coveting a secret companion – gone is the implicating 'me' and 'my'. The original version explains why Nofriari, in the most private way, persisted in daydreaming: 'During all these fourteen years, I had been waiting for my sun to rise, the sun of perfect human sympathy, the sun of passion, as it is called, not consciously looking out for it – our pride and our ignorance are too great for that – but unconsciously shadowing it in idea' (*ms* p. 264). This sun of passion is absent in the published text: seemingly Florence Nightingale, now an established public figure, no longer yearns for human sympathy – having stifled any desire for it.

The seasoned Florence Nightingale doesn't hold out much hope for women's capacity to achieve, either. Women, she claims, keep quiet about what preoccupies them most, keeping an embarrassed silence: 'Dreaming always, never accomplishing, thus women live, too much ashamed of their dreams they think "romantic", to tell them to be laughed at, if not considered wrong' (*Cassandra* p. 218). This is a long way from Nofriari's regrets on the same subject: 'Dreaming always, never accomplishing, thus I lived, too much ashamed of my dreams I thought were "romantic", to tell them where I knew that they would be laughed at, if not considered wrong'. Until, after fourteen years of solitary dreaming, Nofriari is drained of hope: 'So I lived, till my heart was broken. I am now an old woman at thirty' (*ms* p. 263). This heroine, whose heart breaks at thirty, also dies at thirty – which is perhaps why there is no sign of her in the woman returning from the Crimea a decade later. By this point Florence Nightingale had decided that a woman's suffering is an effect of the general condition of women, and not the fate of any particular woman.

Women die young, not from excessive daydreaming – a kind of love-making in the mind – but from expecting too little: this is Florence Nightingale's later 1860 thesis. Consumed by fantasy, women make too few demands on themselves and the world; likewise the world, in response to this, makes too few demands on them. Between 1850 and 1860 Florence Nightingale's attitude changes dramatically: her problems no longer lie with her own femininity, but with the overall condition of women. Disdainful of her yearning youth, she looks back on it with impatience. By 1860 she is no longer weary of life, she is indignant of it – and so spurred to reform. She has done with romance and with the emotions that love unsettles; instead she is set on forging an identity shaped by outward purpose.

Rather than confronting her youthful despair and finding out what is of value in it, Florence distances herself from it. However this means losing something not easily replaced. Even the brooch that Queen Victoria presents on her return from the Crimea is paltry alongside what she has lost. As often happens, when Florence suppresses her romantic interests she increases her resistance to them – without in any way eliminating them. From this point on the romantic interests that offer themselves she ignores or is irritated by, as opposed to being indifferent to. This is hardly surprising, since although she is strong enough to defend herself against what excites her, she isn't strong enough to overcome the conflict this generates. Her attitude is one of resistance, which means that the imaginative energy required to give up longstanding defences is put into tightening them up.

What is lost in Florence Nightingale's suppression of erotic daydreams lives on in the poetry of her *Cassandra* manuscript. Although the opening paragraph aspires to – without reaching – lyrical heights, its literary ambition is clear:

> The night was mild and dark and cloudy. Nofriari was walking to and fro before the beautiful facade of a Palladian palace. All was still. Not one light shining through the window betrayed the existence of any life stirring within. 'I, I alone am wandering in the bitterness of life without', she said. She went down where, on the glassy dark pond, the long shadows of the girdles of pines, the tops of which seemed to touch heaven, were lying. The swans were sleeping on their little island. Even the Muscatel ducks were not yet awake. But she had suffered so much that she had outlived even the desire to die. (*ms* p. 237)

Rather than opening with this exotic dreamy scene, the published version begins staunchly, with no hint of poetry: 'The voice of one crying in the crowd, "Prepare ye the way of the Lord"'. No hint of a Palladian palace, Muscatel ducks, a death wish, or girdles of pines – just a single voice with a Christian message. Above all, no trace of Nofriari's sensuality, made explicit in the next paragraph of the manuscript.

> She re-entered the palace, and reached her balcony; she threw herself down on its cold pavement, resting her forehead on the low balustrade, and her long hair, of the golden tint which the Venetian painter delighted to honour, bound with gems, radiant in the moonlight, fell over her bare arm on to the rough stone – but hardly for a moment could her energetic nature acquiesce in this humiliated despairing posture. She started up, like the dying lioness who fronts her hunters – and standing at bay, as it were, she bared her forehead to the light breeze, and stretching out her arms, she cried: 'God, to thee alone can I say all. God, hear me. Why didst thou create us, with passion, intellect, and

moral activity – these three – and place us in a state of society where no one of those three can be exercised? (*ms* p. 237)

Not wanting to confuse her request to God with a complaint to man, Nofriari talks directly to God. Like the visitor to the Eumenides cave, Nofriari refuses to face her fate lying down; she stands erect, 'like the dying lioness who confronts her hunters'. However this can't last; after an irate, windy speech she falls silent in a 'reluctance of wounded feeling' – which leaves her brother to fill the gaps of her story (*ms* p. 245).

The reason Nofriari needs her brother to tell her story isn't simply that she dies before the end of it, it is also because she doesn't believe her story is worth telling.

> I do not say that with greater strength of purpose I could not have accomplished something. If I had been a hero, I should not need to tell my story for then all the world would have read it in the mission I should have fulfilled. It is because I am a commonplace, ordinary, every-day character that I tell my tale – because it is the sample of hundreds of lives (or rather deaths) of persons who cannot fight with society, or who unsupported by the sympathies about them, give up their own destiny as not worth the fierce and continued struggle necessary to accomplish it. (*ms p.* 264)

This is a heroine who feels she doesn't exist individually, but as one of many – a cross-section of hundreds of other women. A woman who, without sympathy or inspiration, is without singularity of purpose. This is because women, in this heroine's opinion, are unable to stand up against society or to stand out within it.

Literature is another focus of Nofriari's attacks, mainly because it favours those with heroic and eventful lives. If novels are to tell stories about women like herself – who can neither protest against society nor accept their place in it – a new kind of story is needed. But finally it isn't women's gender that requires their story to be told, nor their failure to act boldly: women need a narrator because, with the collapse of their erotic hopes, they can't be bothered to narrate their own lives. This, Nofriari suggests, is the fate of every woman who spends her youth in a hapless daydream for the perfect partner.

Unlike his sister, Fariseo considers Nofriari's story worth telling – in part to make up for his own incomprehension when she lived:

> I am the brother of poor Nofriari, and I tell her story as she told it me, one day when I blamed her for not finding her happiness in life as I and her contemporaries have done; and she answered that I did not know whether her life had been such that she could either find happiness in it or alter it.

Like the narrator's attitude to 'poor Gwendolen' in *Daniel Deronda*, Fariseo's sympathies cannot be stretched to represent his sister's life. However he does try:

> I made some few notes of our conversation, for it occurred a short time only before her death – My poor sister! She died at thirty – wearied of life, in which she could do nothing, having ceased to live the intellectual life long before she was deserted by the physical life. I saw her on her death-bed . . . giving way to the tears and exclamations natural on such occasions. (*ms* p. 286)

Even Fariseo can see that Nofriari's ambitions were lost well before her illness, as her mind hardened against the hopes that could – had she kept hold – have kept her responsive and alert.

Nofriari dies an old woman, devoid of hope:

> 'Yes', she said to [her brother] one day, 'I feel that my Youth is gone. I used to laugh at the poet's sunny description of the May-time of youth, and say that *I* had never felt anything like that. But now I see the great difference between Youth and Middle-Age. Before, I suffered – but I always thought that I *should* carry out my schemes. I lived but for that. I lived upon desire, upon the dream of my hopes fulfilled. Now I see that I never shall fulfil them. I have lost the vigour of hope – the spell to desire – the sap to dream. I have come even to regret the enjoyments which I thought unworthy of me, even to pick up as I went by. (*ms* p. 270)

This is a woman who no longer believes she can attract a lover. Instead of moving forward from youth to middle-age, Nofriari moves away from spring and fulfilment and toward a barren winter. Without spring, without desire, she is nothing, unworthy even of passing pleasures. This joylessness says more about her particular state of mind than about the condition of mature women; moreover it suggests a satisfaction so precious that it must be withdrawn from awareness.

A woman who is young at heart is in touch with a part of herself that is still in contact with an early loved one; this loved one may be at the back of her mind, but without being suppressed from it. To be youthful one needn't be young: a woman who distances herself from loved ones who were the focus of past pleasures could miss out on youthfulness altogether. When Nofriari lets go of her loved ones, her erotic decline is as unbearable as it is incommunicable. Without 'the spell to desire' she loses touch with the parts of herself that are sustained by links with past loved ones. Like Sarah, Lot's wife, in the Old Testament, something in Nofriari turns to salt and becomes crusty. This is why she looks to an imaginative last resort, her own death, to express her suffering. She takes her life, but passively, in revenge for a loss of goodness and love within.

Just as women's hearts can be broken, so too can their prose. The older Florence Nightingale breaks up Nofriari's story, deleting whole passages and playing down others, presumably for fear of exposure. She takes away the narrative, effaces the heroine, and replaces the poetry with polemic. The thrust of this polemic is that women are without an intellectual and creative destiny; in part this is because women exert themselves at 'odd times' of the day, which means their concentration never lasts longer than a few minutes. As if to confirm this, the narrator jumps from one idea to the next, planting the current state of women at the feet of one and then another problem: their education, or rather lack of it; their mothers, whose resentment for their daughters stems from their own erotic sacrifices; a society which precludes intimacy between lovers and makes marriage a lottery; and a system of courtship in which money rules and women are kept sexually ignorant.

Women tend to love more and accommodate more than men, in Nofriari's opinion, not because they are loving and accommodating by nature, but because they are innocent of the experiences that might qualify their love – 'woman has nothing but her affections, and this makes her at once more loving and less loved' (*Cassandra* p. 224). Women, it follows, are faithful by default, which further skews the relations between the sexes. 'The woman's passion is generally more lasting. It is possible that this difference may be because there is really more in man than in woman. There is nothing in her for him to have this intimate communion with' (*Cassandra* p. 223). Because a woman loves in a vacuum, there is nothing to keep the two lovers together. And yet ultimately something more fundamental than social and educational differences are at fault. Fault ultimately lies in the 'intimate communion' that the woman seeks, originating in an intimacy which goes beyond – and dates prior to – romantic love; and hence interferes with a smooth progress from romance to marriage.

Whereas a woman of twenty daydreams, a woman of thirty suffers; yet both are yearning for a 'sun of a perfect human sympathy' – the younger with longing, the elder with regret. Many realist novelists, including Tolstoy and George Eliot, disapproved of romantic novels – presumably because they climax in an erotic union with a fantasied – hence unreal – other. Nofriari also dismisses novels as romantic poison, with a vehemence which suggests there might be something to fear from them. 'The Novel – what a false idea it is – brings two people through no end of troubles, to make them at last – what? – exclusive for the other – caring alone for one another – "wrapped up", as it is called, in each other – an abyss of binary selfishness' (*ms* p. 163). This romantic preference for the couple is not only harmful, it is loathsome – forcing the author to chop into her sentence with dashes and question marks. The novel, Nofriari continues, throws lovers together in precisely the way that society prevents:

> What are novels? What is the secret charm of every romance that was ever written? The first thing in a good novel is to place the persons together in circumstances which naturally call out for high feelings and thoughts of the character, which afford food for sympathy between them on these points – romantic events they are called. The second is that the heroine has *generally* no family ties (almost *invariably* no mother), or, if she has, these do not interfere with her entire independence. (*Cassandra* p. 208)

The 'secret charm' of novels is their lack of reserve, which makes characters more interesting than they are in reality. A heroine in a novel, who is nearly always independent of family ties, has no need to struggle with the emotional complexities that most girls encounter in family relationships. In Nofriari's mind, family ties cause the worst kind of exploitation: 'the family uses people, *not* for what they are, not for what they are intended to be, but for what it wants them for – for its own uses' (*Cassandra* p. 216). Concerned only with itself, the family can't afford to be genuinely interested in its members. The combined impact of family and society on the female mind, she finishes, is always harmful – 'the system dooms some minds to incurable infancy, others to silent misery' (*Cassandra* p. 216).

Florence Nightingale is especially attuned to the conflict between inner demands and those of family and society. In Nofriari's view every woman chooses how she deals with family and social pressures – either by transcending or being crushed by them. Intelligence alone is no advantage; it may even increase a woman's struggle, since 'the more complete a woman's organisation the more she will feel' the pressures on her. This situation isn't destined to last, however, since 'there will come a woman who will resume in her own soul, all the sufferings of her race, and that woman will be the Saviour of her race' (*ms* p. 279). This will be no ordinary woman, vulnerable to the knocks of daily life. But where might this Saviour come from, she asks herself, given that no-one seems to fit this description? 'The next Christ will be a female Christ – I believe. But I do not see one woman who looks like a female Christ. I don't see anyone who looks, in the least, like her Precursor even. If I could see one, I would be the messenger before her face, to go before her and prepare the hearts and minds for her' (*ms* p. 284). Rather than being a saviour herself, Nofriari would rather be her servant, finding inspiration – and release – this way.

The tragedy for Nofriari – and for women like her – is that she can't wait for a saviour, so desperate is she 'for reality and for hope' now. When Nofriari dies of starvation – mentally not physically – the surrounding world can only watch and stare:

> To have no food for our heads, no food for our hearts, no food for our activity, is that nothing? If we have no food for the body, how we do cry out, how all the world hears of it, how all the newspapers talk of it, with a paragraph headed in great letters,

DEATH FROM STARVATION! But suppose one were to put a paragraph in the 'Times', *Death of Thought from Starvation*, or *Death
of Moral Activity from Starvation*, how people would stare, how
they would laugh and wonder! (*Cassandra*, p. 220).

Just as in extreme hunger the stomach starts ingesting
itself, a woman's mind that hasn't been fed turns back on
itself and attacks the mechanisms that – in better circum-
stances – sustain it. But apart from conflating food as a
symbol of nourishment and mental stimulus, what does this
paragraph from the *Times* tell us? Do women really depend
on the world so entirely, such that without it they would
starve? Is there, within each woman, nothing that can
generate her own well-being?

At the climax of *Cassandra* the heroine appeals to an
indifferent world one last time:

Oh! Call me no more Nofriari, call me Cassandra. For I have
preached and prophesied in vain. I have gone about crying all
those many years, Wo to the people! And no-one has listened or
believed. And now I cry, Wo to myself! For upon me destruction
has come. (*ms* p. 271)

In the published version Florence thinks better of including
this passage, even though it explains her heroine's suffering
and the myth behind it. Nofriari, like Cassandra before her,
dies because her warnings are unheeded. And yet she
protests too much; even though her warnings are ignored
this isn't enough to cause her death. Ultimately Nofriari
neither takes her own life nor has it taken from her. Among
her last words, again removed, are three short sentences:
'The glory has departed. The life has gone out of me. I recognise my existence but by suffering' (*ms* p. 263). Here there is
no assailant, only a painful shift from youthful daydreaming
to middle-aged suffering. What was once a life of romantic
pleasures has become a misery that bears no quality, no
narrative, no rhythm – just wordless pain. After being
pursued by her own furies to give up her erotic daydreams,
Nofriari dies of depression. Her powers of prophecy may
have been overlooked, but it is the frustration of her wish to
be loved that finally kills her – this is why she can 'neither
find happiness in life nor alter it'.

This novel begs further questions. What was Florence's
aim in placing *Cassandra* inside the privately published

Suggestions for Thought, sent to six eminent public figures – none of them women – including J.S. Mill, Benjamin Jowett, and her father W.E. Nightingale? What is the connection between a heroine who prophesies in vain, and an author who reviles her own privilege? Does Nofriari fulfil or martyr herself in death? And lastly what causes her death, society's indifference or her author's rage?

Cassandra is no artless tale; whatever other aims it satisfies, it is a message to interested parties. Nofriari ultimately appeals to God, however Florence Nightingale made it clear that religion always involves the family – 'the two questions concerning the relation to God and the relation to the parent are one'.[6] On preparing to leave her family, Florence wrote of her anguish in a private note – 'there are knots which are Gordion and can only be cut'.[7] What better way to cut family ties than to write a story that highlights the suicidal risk of not doing so? And what could be more dramatic than to project this conflict on to a myth which obscures it? Moreover within her family it wasn't only Florence who was drawn to this myth: her sister Parthenope, under her married name Lady Frances Verney, also called the heroine of her first novel, *Stone Edge*, Cassandra.

Florence Nightingale uses the myth of Cassandra to confront a vision of early death and to awaken a desire for life beyond her family. This myth shocks her out of vain protest: Cassandra's fate is Florence's nightmare – terrifying, prophetic, and yet in a final and unthinkable sense, pleasurable. This makes *Cassandra* distinct from other novels considered in this book. Essentially it tells the story of a woman's mind, drained of energy, dominated by the need to give up both pleasures and loved ones – hence its wilful and at times claustrophobic qualities. Nofriari's suffering is the story of a rebellion gone wrong, for reasons her brother can't fathom. He cannot see that once his sister has internalised her struggle with a loved one, her struggle is endless, since she is now loyal to a part of herself that she can't break free of, however fiercely she tries.

Nofriari becomes hysterical the moment she gives up on romantic love. This could be why her thoughts on marriage sound like an ultimatum: 'I felt that I must choose, either to hold myself ready to sacrifice, *if* called upon, feelings, religious, social, political (but when these were all gone, there would not be much of me left) or I must sacrifice love and marriage. I preferred the latter' (*ms* p. 266). But then in the next passage Nofriari's sacrifice is less clear, especially when her memories of a lover's slight upsets her poetic flight:

> Oh! How cruel are the revulsions which high-minded women suffer. I remember, at the ruins of Palmyra, amid the wrecks of worlds and palaces and temples, thinking of one who I had loved in connection with great deeds, noble thoughts, devoted feelings. I saw the man again. It was at one of those crowded parties of Civilisation which we call Society. His only careless passing remark was, 'The buzz tonight is like a manufactory.' Yet that man loved me still. (*ms* p. 278)

Nofriari's dilemma is less that of making herself heard at a crowded party, than of absorbing this man's indifference. And yet this man – whom she insists loves her still – is absent from the final version.

Ultimately it is easier – it generates less resistance – for Nofriari to lament the fate of womankind, than to despair her own fate. It is easier for her to mourn a general good – an equal relation between the sexes – than to admit the ruin of her hopes for love. However much she regrets the absence of a female spirit, it is her own affair she is suffering in this next unpublished passage:

> Oh! Miserable fate of the woman! It seems to me, when I hear that eternal wind sighing and lamenting I know not where as if the female spirit of the world were mourning everlastingly, over blessings – not lost, but which she has never had – and which, in her discouragement, she feels that she never will have, they are so far off. (*ms* p. 279)

Her lament may seem vague, but her longing is not. The female spirit she appeals to is universal, dooming all women to short emotional lives. However this spirit is too general, when in fact Nofriari gives up on life because she gives up on love, and this for the most personal of reasons.

As distinct from the myth in which Cassandra is slain by a ruthless Clytemnestra, Nofriari dies by no-one's hand, 'her mourners' standing by. And unlike Cassandra, whose prophecies are spoken to the wind, Nofriari's last words are recorded by her brother. The tone of her parting words may be sad, but an ecstasy shines through them.

> She lay for some time silent. Then starting up and standing upright – for the first time for many months, she stretched out her arms and cried, 'Free – free – oh! divine freedom, art thou come at last? Welcome, beautiful death!' She fell forward on her face. She was dead. (*ms* p. 281)

This may not be great literature, but it is remarkable for its blend of excitement and pathos. Conflict falls away, uncertainty ends, and Nofriari welcomes death as a release. Nofriari – and perhaps her author – is in thrall less to a hostile social world than to feelings so strong that they can't be brought back as memories and so put to rest. Instead they persist in isolated parts of the heroine's mind, finding expression in melancholy protest. The way forward for this heroine, an alternative to suicide, would have been to recall these memories with the aim of absorbing – rather than rejecting – the feelings they bring with them. Again, in the words of Robert Frost, 'the best way out is always through'.

However perseverance is not given to Nofriari – a woman 'who sees the veil [others] do not see, and yet has no power to discover the remedy for it' (*Cassandra*, p. 205). Were she strong enough to return to her painful feelings and to find words for them, she would be able to reflect on them *as* memories, rather than emotional triggers. However Nofriari is without this strength, which is why when a lover passes her over she simply refuses to think about him. In this way her threshold for conflict is lowered and her defences stepped up, which means – in turn – that although she has insights others lack, she is powerless to act on them.

This is a heroine who would rather do battle with anxiety than give in to depression. 'Give us back our suffering, we cry to Heaven in our hearts – suffering rather than indifferentism; for out of nothing comes nothing. But out of suffering may come the cure'. Better an active life of suffering than a quiet life of looking on. 'A hundred struggle and drown in the breakers. One discovers the new world. But rather, ten times rather, die in the surf, heralding the way to that new world, than stand idly on the shore!' (*Cassandra* p. 208). Anxiety – the release of tension in the expectation of danger – is to be a 'hundred times' preferred over 'standing idly on the shore'.

However the conditions responsible for women standing idly by are only secondarily bound up with social, family, and educational issues. Women are not more easily depressed than men because they have found it difficult to gain equal social rights and access to higher education. Women are easily depressed because they are inclined to interpret real difficulties, like these, in a personal way. Having been brought up to respect inherently masculine ideals, only to realise they can't live up to them, the self-esteem of a number of women wanes. Nofriari wouldn't have been depressed by her family's indifference to her ambitions had she herself supported them unequivocally; that is, if she hadn't needed their support to realise them in the first place.

Florence Nightingale's view of the struggle between the sexes is developmental: men get a better time of it, not because of an essential difference or superiority, but because their ambitions are less warped during adolescence. From an early age, women are prey to frustrations and losses of confidence they are powerless to prevent. Men tend to escape these frustrations, she suggests, not because they handle reality more easily, but because their personalities survive their upbringing intact. Florence is critical of a society that fans the interests of men while pressing down on women and so compromising their interests. In her opinion, women are easily depressed because they look outside for confirmation of their self-esteem, with the result that when it is lacking outside they withhold it inside. A way out of this dilemma – the one Florence chose – is to identify with masculine aims which convey their own sense of credit. No wonder, then, that she primed herself for war and became indispensable when she got there – given the significance of war as a symbol of masculine achievement.

The *condition* of women – or men for that matter – has a double meaning: it refers firstly to a specific quality of one's being, and secondly to constraint common to a group or class. These meanings are distinct, yet they slide into each other in common use. It is one thing to talk about a condition of one's being, like a vulnerability to depression, and quite another to talk about a historical constraint on women, like a bar to women owning property. When Nofriari becomes hysterical it is for internal reasons, rather than the external reasons she blames; the constraint on her freedom may become synonymous with the conflict in her mind, but it can't in itself explain it. While the impulse to map internal conflicts on to social causes is understandable – especially since it provides a general account for conflicts which might otherwise elude understanding – the specificity of a woman's unhappiness will always demand more, descriptively and analytically, than a general explanation can give.

When Nofriari gets depressed, she starts blaming herself for not being able to attract the one she loves – not the world who made women passive in courtship. Unlike her anxiety for an imaginary danger in the future, her depression treats this danger as past – any damage is done already, hence her helplessness before it. As despair creeps into her thoughts, all talk of being saved, or of a saviour, disappears. This step is inevitable psychologically. If despair is to communicate something more than a lament, it needs the recognition of a close intimate. Nofriari never gets this support; even her brother's interest comes too late. Instead she finds her strength in resistance; in holding out against excitement and in not falling for erotic longing. In this she is successful, even if this success turns out to be futile.

Having suppressed her love to the point of forgetting she ever felt it, Nofriari becomes brittle – shrill even. Protest, a reversal of longing, can be as unattractive in an older woman as longing is attractive in a younger woman. In refusing to give way to erotic longing Nofriari effectively forgets – loses touch with – the memories that her well-being and youthfulness rely on. Hence she really does die of starvation – of a protest which eats away at what is most important to her – leaving her with nothing.

The author of *Cassandra* is finally too hysterical to be a novelist. Having repressed her desire for an 'accidental means for unrestrained communion', Florence avoids any reminder of it. She has too much at stake to empathise with the imaginative vulnerabilities of others, or to stay on the noisy path of narrative with its compositional and stylistic demands. She suffers too keenly from her own hysteria to represent this potential in another, and so fails as an author. Ultimately she fails because of her fear of creativity, as expressed in her self-loathing. This makes *Cassandra* an elaborate hoax, genuine in appeal but hollow in purpose; it is aimed at damning the world, rather than saving it. More of a sketch of a novel than a novel, *Cassandra* mirrors Florence's own equivocal relation to life. After all, how can you create if you hate creativity?

Notes

1. Florence Nightingale's Diary, 1 June 1850. Quoted by Donald R. Allen, in 'Florence Nightingale: Toward a Psychohistorical Interpretation', *Journal of Interdisciplinary History*, Summer 1975, no. 6, pp. 23–54, p. 30.
2. Lytton Strachey, *Eminent Victorians* (Penguin, 1918, 1948) pp. 111–162.
3. Florence Nightingale, *Suggestions for Thought and Cassandra*, edited by Mary Poovey (Chatto and Pickering, 1992) p. 226. Further quotations will appear in the text as *Cassandra*.
4. George Eliot, *Middlemarch*, edited by Barbara Hardy (Penguin, 1980) p. 25.
5. Manuscript of *Suggestions for Thought*, British Library Manuscripts, Add. 45839, p. 264. Further quotations from the manuscript are given in the text as *ms*.
6. Florence Nightingale, *Suggestions for Thought* (Eyre and Spottiswoode, 1860) vol. 2, p. 245.
7. *Notes from the Devotional Authors of the Middle Ages, collected, chosen and freely translated by Florence Nightingale (1872–93)*, British Library Manuscripts, Add. 45841, p. 17.

7

Femininity Against Itself

If you go to the National Gallery in London, and venture into the twentieth-century rooms, you will see a smallish portrait of Madame Cezanne. Although it is one of many portraits that Cezanne did of his wife, this one is special. Her head is slightly cocked, as if in query, yet without any expectation of an answer. The brush strokes of her dress, in blue green swirls, are unfinished, suggesting that it could have been any dress that she wore for the sitting. How is it that her face could be so expressive, and yet give so little of herself away? Even if one knows nothing about Madame Cezanne's personal history, a whole world of small sufferings can be seen in her face. While it is fine not to smile, one has the feeling that Madame Cezanne couldn't smile, not fully. Her face muscles have been pulled downward, so that over the years her cheeks have taken on this fixed look.

There is a familiar story which can be told about women such as Madame Cezanne – a story which makes her into the victim of a remorseless male demand, sucking the life from her in pursuit of her husband's project. And how do women end up in unsatisfactory debilitating relationships? Lack of opportunity, lack of a social framework in which to conceive and realise their own creative projects? But however much truth there may sometimes be in such explanations, they run the risk of veiling something more complex and more disturbing.

Henry James' *Portrait of a Lady* can be read as an experiment with just such a situation. The heroine, Isabel Archer, is deliberately set up with every opportunity. The machinations of her cousin, Ralph Touchett, lead to her inheriting her uncle's banking fortune. The novelist then takes her to Italy to present her with benign imaginative space in which to piece together her own concerns and to develop her own projects. But while there she is drawn into a relationship – and eventually marriage – with a man who seeks only to crush her and use her money to satisfy his own desperate fantasy of distinction. But why does Isabel marry this 'sterile aesthete', as Ralph bitterly describes him in an attempt to head Isabel off from a disastrous alliance. It is true that Isabel has something which others covet – money; but she also has grace, beauty, and vitality which, wherever they appear, are coveted by others.

None of this, however, explains Isabel's compliance – that another desires something one has is no sufficient reason for giving it to them on a plate. Isabel's problem, it seems, is that *she* can't think what to do with herself and so positively gives herself up to another's greed. The marriage is all the more cruel because Isabel had lately refused an offer of marriage from Lord Warburton. This refusal is especially poignant in the film version, where Lord Warburton comes across – even more than in the novel – as a deeply nice man. What the first suitor lacked – for Isabel's agreement – was grasping, confident insistence. Gilbert Osmond (the sterile aesthete) doesn't seduce, doesn't plead, he just insists that Isabel must marry her. It is the egoistic urgency of his demands which she follows.

Although James makes the pathos of the situation richly apparent, he provides no convincing account of why Isabel should be attracted to this kind of selfish insistence. What I have tried to do in this book is put together a feminine psychology which yields insights into fates like that of Isabel Archer. And which shows the kinship of Isabel and Madame Cezanne and millions of 'ordinary' women. Isabel's money – her great freedom on manoeuvre – simply stands as an unusually clean and clear example of a more general phenomenon: capacities unused, opportunities unrealised. This psychology has emerged touch by touch from the consideration of cases as presented in the imaginative, yet realist, literature of the nineteenth century.

But to hazard summation, the view which emerges is this. For a great many women, a sense of their own promise along with possession of the force required to realise that promise, develops in the orbit of love, and particularly in the orbit of a father's love – a love which is an amalgam of reality and fantasy. When this father dies, or (less dramatically) when he is cut down in imagination or placed in a harsher, less flattering, conception of the world (which experience can hardly fail to produce) the girl falters. Where, now, are her ideals? How, now, is she to go forward? And so her capacity to engage with the world is undermined and she begins to despair of herself.

Having put her faith in an ideal, such a girl is left to deal with reality. I have traced the cases in which something troubling happens in response to this initial crisis: hysteria and reactive femininity. At first a girl may retain, in imagination, the possibility of the perfect father – on whom her self-confidence depends. She continues to judge and desire by the standards set in her early adoring relationship. This immature image turns the world into a place of continual shocks and disappointments. At the same time she may feel compelled to enter a relationship in which she takes up in the position of a child. And this seems to be what happens to Isabel Archer. The problem with Lord Warburton is that he solicits her as someone who is an adult, as a partner, as someone whose personality or point of view might be called upon. By contrast Gilbert Osmond makes no appeal. He simply presents a conception of the world in which Isabel will be permanently an inferior (permanently lagging behind his cultural super-refinement, continually naive and gauche – continually a child in need of being brought up properly). It is this which wins her allegiance because it coincides – however painfully – with her own grasp of herself.

Unlike many women, Rebecca West in Ibsen's *Rosmersholm* is alive to the negative impulses that have the power to fix her expression hard. She obeys harsh thoughts of which she is hardly aware, half knowing she risks death by doing so. In the end Rebecca decides the only course open to her is suicide, jumping off the same bridge she earlier encouraged Rosmer's wife to jump from. At this moment she is elated – not happy, but intensely relieved to have found a way of stopping her damning thoughts forever. Had Rebecca not acted on this impulse, hadn't died young, she would probably have gone on to turn her hysterical thoughts into reactive ones – turning from a girl who can't bear to have certain desires into a woman who can't afford to have them at all.

When a woman silently agrees with her unspoken – often harsh – thoughts she soon comes to think badly of herself. Suppressed thoughts tend to be overwhelmingly negative or, occasionally, grandly positive – which is why they are suppressed in the first place. This explains why a woman who feels she is unworthy of love looks in vain for a lover who will value her: since even if she meets someone who appreciates her, her self-belittling thoughts will block her lover's praises. At the other extreme a woman may assume she is too good to be loved, which is why no man is worthy of her, all lovers are slaves, and every romance falls short.

Although Sue Bridehead in Thomas Hardy's *Jude the Obscure* never kills herself, certainly she kills her love for Jude – as do a number of women as they mature. It is almost as if a woman needs to sustain certain conditions for loving if she is *not* going to kill her love. Dominated by thoughts pushed to the edge of awareness, Sue is unable to accept Jude's love and quickly becomes reactively feminine. Despite her intention to be true to their love, she obeys thoughts which prevent their relationship developing. Because she is hardly aware of her harmful thoughts she never articulates them in a way that might transform them. Jude, on his side, is perplexed by a force in Sue that is only satisfied by their shared unhappiness. Ironically Jude finds it harder to help Sue, who goes out of her way to disguise her distress, than his first wife Arabella, who appeals to him openly. By the end of the novel Jude is living with the worst of both worlds, a hysterical first wife and a reactively-feminine second wife – which could be why many readers find the novel hard-going.

With passing years Sue Bridehead, Olive Chancellor, and Isabel Archer all react to pressures in a way which leads to their avoidance of intense excitement. This has a number of effects: it encourages them to stop following their most powerful thoughts through; it causes them to curb their interest in people they find threatening or exciting; and it pushes them to conceal their hands – their aims – from others. This makes them enigmatic to others who fail to see that they are dominated by defences which provide a strange sort of pleasure. Although Isabel Archer doesn't enjoy her suffering, she does experience it as meaningful, which is a distinct kind of pleasure. Suffering becomes essential to Isabel as, over time, it becomes part of her identity. This shift is made by numerous women, now as then, who come to recognise themselves as sufferers. While their distress is real, so is the pleasurable relief their suffering brings – hence their attachment to suffering. This is the link that Isabel's longstanding American lover finds it impossible to break: he can't understand how it is that Isabel's pleasure, suffering, and identity can be so closely knit that any demand he makes only increases her need to suffer.

A girl who refuses to be the kind of girl she thinks others expect her to be, is distinct from a woman who denies her womanliness. Whereas a mixed-up girl may make herself too thin to be attractive, and count this a success, a woman under inner pressure will act differently – perhaps by identifying with the functional or maternal aspects of herself, and ignoring the passionate and ambitious aspects. A skinny girl makes an indirect yet open protest against her femininity; in contrast a practical, motherly woman conceals her protest beneath a seeming maturity – denying herself pleasures with a conviction that others are taken in by, never suspecting it belies a suppressed wish. A woman who obscures her desires in this way presents a particular challenge, mainly because, having suppressed her desires, they can only be inferred. This is why it is harder to help a woman who leaves others to guess at her suffering, than a girl who is – often despite herself – eager to give clues to hers.

Even once a woman's distress has been shared, and her wishes acknowledged, more has to happen before she regains a sense of well-being. This part of the process – which has a two-steps-forward, one-step-back movement – is often underestimated. Unlike a hysterical refusal, which can be reversed, sometimes to miraculous effect, a reactive denial has to be overcome again and again before it dissolves. As I have stressed, because a denial lies outside awareness it can rarely be overcome single-handed – ordinarily someone else is needed to overcome it. Moreover, because of the threat this assistance implies, most women will refuse it until they absolutely need it. Isabel Archer opposes all offers of help until her position becomes impossible; in her case, what looked like pride, turns out to be a reluctance to confide her own helplessness. Throughout her married years in Florence she avoids intimacy, yet she longs for it in her thoughts; but however much she may want Ralph's confidence, she can't bring herself to ask for it. One of James' great insights is that there are often two people – here Isabel Archer and Ralph Touchett – who are ideally placed to help one another, who yet realise their significance to each other too late.

When Ralph Touchett transforms Isabel Archer's fortunes in Jane Campion's film *Portrait of a Lady*, his love for her is plain. Unlike the novel, Isabel eventually admits her love for Ralph, as he does his for her. The film makes a bold move that James himself never makes, which is to overturn Isabel's denials, reawakening her to her own pleasures and interests. The ending of the film shows a self-possessed heroine who, while choosing to return to Italy, does so knowingly. In the novel James presents a more complicated heroine: he seems to know that a woman of Isabel's depth would need to undergo profound changes before her natural responses returned. She would have to take responsibility for an 'I' – as Isabel Archer in her own right, over and above the position of 'she' assigned to her as Gilbert Osmond's wife and the Touchett heiress. This involves representing her experience positively, and so giving definite shape to her inner world. These moves may seem straightforward, and could be, were it not for the conflict they generate in her. To overcome this conflict, she would need to absorb it squarely, without resorting to further defences. The temptation to defend herself from her own turmoil is real, which is why she needs Ralph's support. When, in the novel, Ralph finally dies, Isabel's future is left open; it isn't clear whether she has won her independence in accepting his love for her, or whether she returns to Osmond in the spirit of abandonment.

If a woman like Isabel Archer is to respond positively to the thoughts and feelings that fill her mind, she has to be able to follow one thought through to the next, without blocking particular thoughts. Not only this, she needs to be interested in her thoughts *as* thoughts if she is to recognise the links between them. James is adept at showing how Isabel's sense of herself – and our understanding of her – arises from the thoughts that go through her mind, as distinct from the impression she makes on others. During the fireside scene in Florence, during which Isabel realises the degree of her past self-deception, her thoughts follow their own lead; hours later, cold from an ash-filled fire, she looks on the world with new understanding. For a moment she is Isabel Archer, as opposed to Gilbert's wife or the Touchett heiress. After this dawn in which she lets her thoughts wander, Isabel sees a common thread between the different phases of her life and in this way makes them her own.

A woman who recognises the thread of her life, and who assumes a clear sense of self, has achieved something psychologically – as opposed to clearing a developmental hurdle. However these achievements, being psychological, can always be reversed or lost – they are not permanently given. Whereas a woman who doesn't understand the immune system can, having been given antibiotics for an infection, expect to be well in a week, a woman who lacks self-awareness is unlikely to recover from inner conflict. For an imaginative recovery to be lasting there has to be personal involvement: a woman can be told at length whatever she has been keeping out of awareness and is in her interest to know, without this having any lasting effect on her. Her informant has failed to notice that she is using her suffering to cushion her own destructiveness. This is why she suppresses her strong thoughts and feelings – out of sight, out of mind – and considers her suffering a small price to pay for keeping them elsewhere.

Henry James describes Olive Chancellor in *The Bostonians* as mature – but by whose measure? Olive is attracted to Verena Tarrant, a younger woman whom she enjoys considerable power over. Olive soon gives herself away as reactive rather than mature: because she wants things from Verena that she can't admit wanting – youth, beauty, sexuality – she has to become devious in getting them. As a woman Olive Chancellor is hard to like; she shuns intimacy and stands aloof from others, yet is drawn to those who enjoy close relations. As Olive's story gathers pace her inability to respond sensitively and intelligently to her strong feelings, without rejecting them out of hand, becomes apparent. As is often the case, Olive's emotional immaturity has little relation to her appearance, her intellect, and her social role which are all well-developed. As long as she dismisses her sexual interest in Verena and her rivalry with Basil Ransom, Olive cannot mature; simply because in dismissing these impulses she distances herself from the kinds of experiences which might mature her.

Isabel Archer begs similar questions. *Portrait of a Lady* revolves around Ralph Touchett's fantasy of a privileged femininity, a fantasy that inspires him to free Isabel from material constraint. By lifting Isabel above worldly concerns Ralph satisfies his wish to find out what kind of lady she will – in her own right – become. However this wish collapses when Isabel's glorious freedom turns out to be notional: undecided about what kind of woman she would like to be, she attracts a lover who moulds her according to his own vision of womanhood – with the result that she sits for Gilbert Osmond's own portrait of a lady. Is James ironic in his choice of title? Is he suggesting that a lady becomes lady-like through restrictions which narrow her in places where she could have been round? The ending of the novel leaves this matter open. Isabel's decision to return to her Italian husband could either be a flash of insight into her needs, or her mistaken responsibility: on whose behalf does she return to Florence, that of her condemning husband or of her own?

Why is it that many women, across time, have feared the worst? And, in fearing the worst, have evaded the kind of intimacy that might help them overcome these fears? An important reason is that a woman who is quietly possessed by negative fantasies is likely to anticipate her release from them as a prelude to inner collapse. After all, why should she want to be liberated from defences which represent her only security? Hence her refusal to accept any help which stands between a stable – if defensive – state of mind, and a promised dissolution of it. Eugenie Grandet, Lucy Snowe, Masha, Gwendolen Harleth, and Nofriari all prefer to keep their defences intact, rather than risk losing them. It would be a rare woman who loosened a defence without being sure there would be something in place to support her, once she had let go of it. Rising above this impulse takes special courage – which is precisely what a woman who feels vulnerable is likely to lack.

When a girl who feels hysterical rejects the one she loves, the strength of her rejection reflects the longing – never quite suppressed – she yet feels for him (or her). In contrast when a reactively-feminine woman rejects the one she loves, she also suppresses her longing, which is why there is often no outward sign of her interest. This puts her at a further disadvantage, since without an awareness of her longing for someone special, it is hard for her to feel good about everyone else. Moreover, and here it gets complicated, it is only after she has admitted to this longing that she can deal with the conflict that went with her earlier experience of longing.

Sue Bridehead never confesses her longing for Jude and, in her attempt to smother it, clearly suffers. And yet she is considered a New Woman; that is, a woman liberated from conventions – inner and outer – of the period. However liberation from social conventions and release from inhibitions are not identical. The narrator in *Cassandra* notes how 'woman's inward development and outward activity do not keep parallel now': a woman's advances in the world, she suggests, needn't bring with it psychological ones. Every liberation is a liberation from something, and what a woman who responds hysterically or reactively to life seeks liberation from are the tensions which fill her own mind. It was futile for Ralph Touchett to encourage his father to leave Isabel Archer an inheritance, until she had resolved the inner struggles that would allow her to enjoy it. Nor is it helpful for Jude to ask Sue to live openly with him, until she has come to terms with her own disapproval of free love. Only slowly and painfully does Jude realise that before Sue can love him despite the rule of society, she needs to release herself from the rule of her conscience. Jude can't effect this on Sue's behalf – any more than can Ralph for Isabel. Despite advances in the external conditions of women, whether in the last or this century, a woman's well-being has to be won over and again – with help – for herself.

On the surface Sue Bridehead seeks a good and happy life for herself; this, however, has to be squared with her drive for the worst, suggestive of a neurotic debt. Although Sue tries to do and to be good, all the while she thinks something dreadful is about to happen – which it does. Similarly, Gwendolen Harleth longs for goodness, yet never ceases guarding others from her wickedness; Lucy Snowe founds a school in her fiancé's honour, an openly hopeful aim, even though she's convinced he won't return; Masha pours love into her baby, and at the same time pushes her husband away; while Nofriari, claiming she is dying on behalf of all women, in the next breath condemns them as a class. In all these positive strivings there is a negative impulse at work; possibly because whenever satisfactions are directed away from one's self and lived out through others, frustration is never far away.

Frustration is a dangerous source of energy; although it can achieve similar aims to those of pleasure its effects are quite different. A woman who feels frustrated tends to project the satisfaction she herself desires on to another, so that she then resents their enjoyment of it. This is what happens to Olive Chancellor when she meets Verena Tarrant in James' *The Bostonians*: entranced by Verena's flair as a public speaker, Olive is also infuriated by Verena's success, wanting it for her own. Subject to frustration of this kind a woman cannot win: Olive admires her young friend and yet resents her – while despairing of herself. Like Sue Bridehead and numerous other women, Olive spends her life paying off an undeclared debt that – being undeclared – is never paid.

Far from being weakened by mental conflict, the heroines in this book share a remarkable strength of will and conscience – as if their experience of conflict makes them strong. At first hysteria protects them from the strong feelings that a lover's presence excites in them; eventually, however, this erotic conflict is transformed into a general mental conflict. When a lover is taken into a woman's mind he (or she) undergoes irreversible change: having been imaginatively absorbed, the lover soon becomes distinct from an actual person. This is because he (or she) is assimilated on the model of early loved ones – with all the associated hopes, wishes, and fears that go with this. However quiet and unassuming Verena Tarrant may outwardly be, after being taken up by Olive Chancellor, the reader's sense of her is coloured by Olive's feelings for her. When Olive loses Verena to Basil Ransome, her memory of Verena is shaped by the feelings and fantasies the younger woman awakens in her. Alternatively, a lover who is valued for his kindness could become a fearful inner presence – even a persecutory one – if his kindness prompts strong negative feelings – of guilt, perhaps – in his partner. Although these processes are hard to grasp, one thing is certain: the lover who returns to haunt – or to bless – a woman, is never the same as the lover who was lost.

When a struggle with a loved one is long and bitter, sometimes its only imaginable end is death. Certainly death plays a decisive role in many realist novels as a climactic 'too late'. This deathliness takes various forms: nostalgic melancholy in *Eugenie Grandet*, a ghostly nun in *Villette*, uncanny reminders in *Family Happiness*, morbid fear in *Daniel Deronda*, and a suicide bid in *Cassandra*. These are attempts to end an unbearable struggle in the heroine's mind; but not just this, they are also attempts to give what is otherwise unthinkable imaginative shape. In an interview with George Eliot, the Russian critic Sofia Kovalevskaya asked why so many of her novels end in death. Without hesitating, Eliot replied:

> There is some truth in what you say; but I'd like to ask you one thing. Have you really not noticed that it actually happens that way in life? I personally refuse to believe that death is not more logical than one usually thinks. When a situation in life becomes more tense, when one cannot see a way out anywhere, when the most sacred duties conflict, then death appears, suddenly opening new ways about which no one had thought before, and reconciles that which had seemed irreconcilable. It has already happened so many times that faith in death has given me courage to live![2]

These 'new ways' which can hardly be thought about – requiring a double negative to express them – are essential

to George Eliot's philosophy of life. For her death is a character – 'then death appears' – who plays a decisive role in
putting an end to messy personal conflicts. However, while
death has the power to end a woman's struggles, it cannot, I
would add, resolve them. When a woman's anger toward a
loved one is at odds with her loyalty for them, a clash is
inevitable. Should this clash deepen, she will be split
between opposite impulses – between loyally wanting to take
in and possess her loved one forever, and angrily wanting to
do away with him (or her), so as to be rid of an impossible
tension. Killing off someone that inspires this conflict is
however no answer, since the conflict lives on in fantasy,
regardless.

Those who suffer in this way are sensitive to the mixed
nature, good and bad, of feelings relating to a loved one. A
girl who feels hysterical does her best to free herself of
intense excitement, but fails; a woman who reacts against
her femininity is more successful, but by being so, she
protects herself from *every* exciting stimulus, regardless of
its potential value for her. The result is often a reactive sense
of goodness, based on the exclusion of excitement. A woman
who reacts in this way is too good, in the righteous sense, to
be true to her desires, some of which she perceives as
improper. Such a woman is uncomfortable to be with, since
the mixture of goodness and righteousness gives her a fatal-
istic – sometimes even a morbid – tinge. She forgets that the
avoidance of excitement is futile, since no defence can keep
out excitement that wells up from within.

A woman who is preoccupied with being good is usually
concerned, at a deeper level, with the consequences of being
bad. However it is not the fear of being bad that is the root of
her suffering. In the opinion of the priest in Balzac's 'A
Woman of Thirty', it is not wrong-doing which lies behind
women's suffering, but erotic neglect. (As ever, I mean erotic
in the broadest sense, that one has the capacity to make
good things happen.) In Balzac's story a troubled
Marchioness seeks out a priest to whom she pours out her
troubles. He replies, swift and sure: 'No, madam, you will
not die of the sorrow that afflicts you and is written on your
features . . . We die not so much from the effects of regrets
as from those of disappointed hopes' (Chapter 2, p. 97). The

Marchioness, as many mature women, suffers more from wishes she hasn't fulfilled, rather than from what she wishes she hadn't done. However deep her remorse, this can't explain her melancholy: ultimately it is her suppressed wishes – her disappointed hopes – that make her feel old at thirty.

A woman who reacts to her femininity will, as she gets older, let slip her erotic hopes. Cassandra dies because she can't direct hostile feelings away from herself, despite remaining free of illness: it is not physical distress that kills her so much as lack of erotic aspiration. When recovering from the impulse to react against one's femininity, it isn't enough to be free of symptoms; complete recovery relies on something harder to effect – the re-establishment of hope. Without expectation and desire, any recovery is partial. A woman who hopes for the best, while quietly thinking the worst, inevitably qualifies the kind of hope she is capable of. A girl who is being hysterical is divided against herself, wanting something in one part of her mind that is contradicted in another. A woman who is reacting to her femininity is also divided, but differently: unaware that one part of her wants something another part frowns on, she is preoccupied with allaying the conflict arising from this split.

For a woman to regain her hope that the undared-for yet wished-for is possible, she has to be willing to daydream. She has to suspend everything she has already experienced and known, to make room for possibilities with little bearing on reality. Daydreams express a spirit of adventure and depend on a willingness to put aside inner standards. When Gwendolen Harleth shrugs off her mother's concern at her ever marrying, given her daughter's cynical attitude to men, Gwendolen retorts, 'I'm not talking about reality, mamma' – a throwaway remark which emphasises how little reality has to do with her strong feelings. At this point in her story Gwendolen is still hopeful, even jaunty, whereas by its end she is without hope. As the novel draws to a close she faces specific challenges: to find ways of giving herself over to pleasure without fearing trouble will follow, and of being generous toward impulses which are at odds with her identity. Ultimately – and this applies to every woman who seeks to regain her well-being – it means opening herself to romance; to overturning her defences and embracing the erotic. It means being open to what she – in reverie – wants, and yet can ill afford – due to strict inner standards – to lay claim to. Above all it means treating the prospect of a 'once more' of satisfaction as alluring, rather than menacing.

The more willingly a woman can make these shifts, the less reactive her femininity will be. By entertaining impulses and memories she first perceives as threatening she will gain in confidence. Moreover if, in daydream, she can allow herself conflictual wishes, her confidence will again increase. Whereas in overcoming hysteria it is useful to discover what a girl desires, with reactive femininity another approach is needed. With an older woman it is less a matter of articulating *what* she may (or may not) desire, than of renewing the vigour with which she desires. While it may be worth asking a girl who is being hysterical what it is she wants, a woman who reacts against her femininity will respond better to being asked what prevents her from wanting at all – for her it is the courage to desire that needs supporting.

Women's attempts to ignore the feelings that inspire conflict is inherently ageing. With time their character becomes fixed in one position and they become brittle. In an early paper Freud explains this as arising from a split between mind and body, which 'is established more readily and is more difficult to remove in women'.[2] Elsewhere Freud compares the mind of a mature woman to 'a stream whose main bed has become blocked' (SE 7 p. 170). A defence which blocks strong impulses has, it seems, brittleness as its outward sign. Freud's response to this phenomenon was pessimistic: he famously shrugged his shoulders over what I am calling reactive femininity. Something about it overtaxed his therapeutic powers, rendering them useless:

> I cannot help mentioning an impression that we are constantly receiving during analytic practice. A man of about thirty strikes us as a youthful, somewhat unformed individual, whom we expect to make powerful use of the possibilities for development opened up to him by analysis. A woman of the same age, however, often frightens us by her psychical rigidity and unchangeability. Her libido has taken up final positions and seems incapable of exchanging them for others. There are no paths open to further development; it is as though the whole process had already run its course and remains thenceforward

insusceptible to influence – as though, indeed, the difficult development to femininity had exhausted the possibilities of the person concerned. As therapists we lament this state of things, even if we succeed in putting an end to our patient's ailment by doing away with her neurotic conflict. (SE7 p.170)

Whereas a man generally enters his maturity at thirty, 'a woman of the same age' is apparently near the end of her development. Freud may lament this contrast but he doesn't elaborate it. This summary of a femininity taken to its logical hard-bitten extreme produces a Medusa-like figure. His mature female patients may be free of symptoms at the end of therapy, but they are not flourishing. However Freud is not the only one to use a set of personality traits gone wrong to describe a mature femininity: Balzac, Charlotte Brontë, Tolstoy, George Eliot, and Florence Nightingale all associate stunted qualities with it.

Everyone knows a Gwendolen Harleth; many women have a touch of Lucy Snowe in them; and most women – at a moment of crisis – fantasise themselves in the role of Cassandra. Any woman can suffer – and make those around her suffer – from inner conflicts she is largely unaware of. Not least because she is in a double mourning: for a feminine essence she has no name for, and for a father who has been lost as a focus of value and love. This father can never return, with the result that the daughter is left to direct the love and hostility – the frustration – this inspires, on to herself, and particularly to her conscience. This increases the hold of her conscience, and excludes her from the understanding that might have been hers had she been able to identify with – rather than simply appeal to – her father.

To the extent that a reactively feminine woman manages to identify with her father, it is with a father who is dead – as an object of erotic interest. However the story doesn't end there. This dead father, it turns out, is a substitute for a living father who refuses to die, and instead goes on living deep inside a woman's mind. (As I have stressed, this kind of love could as well be expressed for a mother, for once she too played a key role for her daughter.) Every lover who descends from this shadowy figure quickly becomes a phantom, which is why every satisfaction is experienced as illusory. To marry a girl bound to a dead father means certain risk. By conflating love itself with her father, this girl (and later this woman) experiences his personal disappearance as a disappearance of love – as an emotional death. This makes her a risk to herself and others, precisely to the degree she turns a blind eye to everything which leads to this conclusion. The brittleness that eventually results doesn't reflect ignorance or stubbornness, but a woman's avoidance of the excitement which allows for flexibility and change. Although this reaction is a common feature of many women, it isn't inherent to femininity. But as the black ice of femininity it exists in many women, and for this reason needs to be understood – not shunned.

The ideal revolution of this ordinary tragedy is an accommodation of reality which enables a girl to love an ordinary, limited, far from perfect father (or to accept that this is what her dead father was) – for such a love is inherently transferable. This then makes it possible for her to accept and feel genuinely supported by a merely good enough lover. (It lowers her standard of 'good enough' to a level which another might actually manage to satisfy.) She can thus find in reality a version of the fantasied support which her childish impression of her father provided. It also allows her to love herself without having to fantasise that she herself is perfect – an immediate release from pressure.

To fail to accommodate reality in this way is to invite trouble. There is nowhere for a woman's development to lead when it is blocked by a refusal to accept life as it is experienced. Although she is still open to learning, all she learns is the misery – and reactiveness – of her position. She gains no vision of how else life could be, is granted no energy or confidence for flight and reconstruction. One aspect of this view of feminine psychology (or rather one of its distinctive features) is that it indicates no easy solutions. It does not suggest that – in this respect – the lot of such women could be improved by athletic or commercial role models, by the creation of more female judges or professors, or by additional resources for child care. This is not to deny the rightness of such demands – merely to question how profoundly such external matters engage with the roots of sadness and anxiety.

A large part of a woman's suffering is imaginative: for example, a woman's response to rejection may spark a humiliation – from years earlier – from which it takes her years to recover. Hysteria – and its later forms – begins in the imagination, develops there, and goes on to use reality as its stage. It is not in the first instance bound up with external conditions. In novel after novel of the nineteenth century the heroine is dominated by strong feelings which she projects on to someone of special significance – usually a lover or parent – whom she can live neither wholly with nor without. These powerful feelings rarely lead her to break down, more often to depression and what I call reactive femininity – a state in which a woman's need for control replaces her desire for pleasure. This is the moment, or series of moments, that I identify in each novel, as the heroine moves from a girlish disappointment, realising the impossibility of her ideals, to a womanly disillusion which confirms it.

Hysteria has a way of calling attention to itself as it – inevitably – fails; hysterical defences are not made to last and their collapse is usually noisy. This period of collapse is crucial, since it brings with it hope of recovery. The way a woman is handled once these defences start loosening reflects important assumptions about the human mind. On the one hand there are psychologists who assume that hysteria indicates an inherent mental weakness, which, being constitutional, can't be corrected. From their point of view the loosening of a woman's defences is a sign that she needs to put more defences in their place, against further conflict. To my mind this is pessimistic. Psychotherapists, on the other hand, tend to see a woman's hysteria as a result of prolonged conflict and excitement – rather than an inherent mental weakness. From a therapeutic point of view we can all be a little hysterical, in that everyone fears they are without what it takes in the sphere of love. Instead of trying to suppress the painful feelings that hysterical defences hold in check, a therapist might encourage a woman to explore them and in this way relieve her distress.

Although a woman needs encouragement if she is to regain her sense of well-being – permission, of sorts – ultimately she herself has to do most of this work. This involves paying attention to the impulses, thoughts, and ideas that pass through her mind – however distressing these may be. There is nothing magical about this process and no quick results are possible. Indeed once Freud and others arrived at this form of treatment, the whole business of therapy became less exciting. The focus shifted away from recalling forgotten memories and toward the dissolving of reminiscences; and it was no longer a matter of tracking down a particular feeling or thought which, once expressed, released a key conflict; rather, it meant a slow, dawning understanding of why excitement and pleasure come to be defended against in later life.

A woman who is feeling hysterical should be encouraged to explore rather than to defend against what excites her. As long as she has no interest in her own excitement, any potential value in it is lost to her. Besides weakening her mentally, this reaction gives her further reason to be fearful of intense pleasures. Nonetheless a woman cannot be persuaded on rational grounds – even of self-interest – to drop her defences. First she has to be convinced, and this takes time, that her inner world is stable enough to risk putting her own pleasure before her need for defence. She has to be persuaded, at a deep level, that the terrible consequences she imagines will follow the giving up of her defences won't happen.

If no attempt is made to lessen a woman's conflict, as the pressures of life mount so will her defences. Should this happen, her natural desire for pleasure will be replaced by an impulse to avoid conflict. This moment is dangerous because, with it, she risks losing her well-being. Without a word being said, a set of denials obscures the excitement which underlay her original need for defence. To say such a woman is afraid of excitement would be misleading. Her fear is more specific; she is afraid of pursuing the kinds of thoughts and feelings that involve loving and hating their object – originally an early loved one. If we accept that our first thoughts and feelings are motivated by wishes for a loved one, some positive and others negative, the process of thinking can't be considered neutral. A woman who becomes hysterical tries to make herself an exception to this rule by restraining her feelings for early loved ones – and every later lover. She reasons that only this way are loved ones safe from feelings which might otherwise possess or destroy them. However in banishing intense feelings she does herself no favours, since once these feelings have been suppressed they can't be linked with conscious feelings and in this way made acceptable.

A woman's fear of imaginatively harming a loved one is mistaken, since those thoughts she considers dangerous are distorted by their origin in childhood fantasies in which only the best and worst possibilities are realised. Not understanding this, she fears the punishment she expects from the rage she once felt for parents who 'only' loved her as a child. As a result, she never stretches her thoughts to the full and feels overwhelmed by her destructive feelings. Ironically it is precisely in restraining her thoughts that she is prevented from overcoming her own destructiveness. As long as she is more concerned about a loved one's survival in her thoughts, than in the thoughts they inspire in her, she will continue to inhibit herself – to hold herself back from the woman she could become.

Without a struggle that disregards – even momentarily – a loved one's survival, there is no appreciation that he (or she) can survive one's attacks. Instead there is the fantasied apprehension, often outside awareness and hence exaggerated, of the loved one's destruction. To relate to others with this fantasy in mind is to engage with them cautiously. In *Studies on Hysteria*, Freud's colleague Breuer recalls how, shortly after the death of Anna O.'s father, Anna walked into the drawing room for tea, only to be struck with 'a particularly terrifying hallucination' of 'her father with a death's head' (SE 2, p. 37). Here Anna's father is transformed – in the most literal way – into a figure of death quite distinct from her dead father. Here is a daughter one might be warned against marrying; a daughter who, having not dared enter a struggle with her father while living, is pursued by him after his death. A woman like Anna O. cannot marry, except in the social sense, as long as she remains locked in this secret embrace with her father.

No girl intends to turn her father into a spectre who comes back to haunt her; however this doesn't mean she is without responsibility should this happen. Eugenie Grandet, one of Balzac's earliest and youngest heroines, is in particular danger when she falls in love for the first time. She loves a man who possesses every quality she would want for herself, but then realises, with growing unhappiness, that he has no intention of sharing these with her. The more eagerly Eugenie sees goodness in Charles, the more she experiences its lack in herself. Believing that through Charles she will discover meaning in her life, Eugenie is quickly drawn to him, only to discover that his own insecurity and self-interest prevents him from loving her. This is a lesson Eugenie never recovers from, which is why his departure signals her loss of hope. When her father dies soon after her lover's departure her sadness turns to melancholy, a shift which is especially hard to reverse.

One reason why our romantic lives become troubled is that, like Rebecca in *Rosmersholm*, we don't willingly give our first loves up. A mother who is dismissed by her daughter will find a way of returning, however determinedly the daughter ignores her. Even when we have done our best to give up our first loves, little can be done against momentary impulses to return them to us. Early loved ones are never completely given up; however secure our attachment to reality, at moments we slip back, if only in daydream and fantasy. These lapses may seem regressive, but this is too simple. Contact with early loved ones remains, throughout life, an important source of hope and expectation, as well as a curb on anxiety and fear. Few of us would take positive steps in reality were they not in contact with loved ones in their imagination. We are all, to the degree we recall these figures, in their debt.

A woman who is thoroughly liberated may find herself at a disadvantage emotionally. Cut off from loved ones in the depths of her mind, staunchly independent of them, she is paradoxically weakened by the boldness of her stand. Sue Bridehead, Rebecca West, and Lucy Snowe are all New Women, even though they experience their independence as both a blessing and a curse. They are free in that they have escaped family ties, but they are also poor, since they have only themselves to turn to. Moreover they are imaginatively preoccupied with maternal figures whom they avoid in their daily lives. While in their personal lives they seek out men, it is as allies, not lovers; at best as partners who are willing, like themselves, to be forgetful of the past.

There is all the difference between a girl who gives up an early loved one knowingly, and hence willingly, and one who does so unknowingly – through repression. If she gives them up willingly, the pleasures and memories inspired by them will stay in her mind; if not, and the most exciting things about them are repressed, hysteria is the likely result. A girl who represses excitement will automatically lose contact with whoever inspired it. It isn't easy to understand why a girl would be willing to let go of the people most important to her. Why fall in with prohibitions that not only frustrate, but wipe out significant memories? She does all these things because she is frightened of the consequences of *not* doing so. More than anything, a girl who becomes hysterical is afraid of the intensity of her wishes, especially those triggered by fantasies about her own family. Such a woman would rather forget everything, the most vivid and warm memories, before giving way to her carefree enjoyment.

All the heroines in this book grow older, but none of them matures; they are all girlish women. Fully ripened, perfectly formed, at the height of development: this is what is usually understood by maturity. Because physical maturity is easier to identify than psychological maturity, what we take to be maturity tends to reflect a full physical flowering. Developed muscles and the potential to reproduce are easy to detect; in contrast, a mind in harmony with itself, fully stretched, is harder to observe. And even when maturity is achieved and mental harmony is reached, it is rarely permanent. This is because maturity concerns the relation to one's inner self, a subtle relation which is effected by parental figures, conscience, and erotic desires. A significant part of maturity reflects the spirit in which an early loved one is absorbed and valued, such that any longing for him (or her) remains in consciousness as a creative rather than a melancholic force. The spirit in which a past love is absorbed is however difficult to detect; access to an individual's thoughts is needed – which is why psychological novels which openly explore the human heart can be so illuminating.

Notes

1. *19th Century Fiction*, Dec. 1978, no. 33, p. 364.
2. Standard Edition of *The Complete Psychological Works of Sigmund Freud*, edited by James Strachey (Hogarth Press, 1953–), vol 3, p.111. Further references to The Standard Edition are given in brackets in the text as SE.

Notes

Since its first version this book has gone through various rewritings, and these End Notes are an opportunity to acknowledge the books that have made my ideas richer. In my comments I have been descriptive rather than summary, in the hope that it will encourage a general reader to browse more widely. A number of titles are no longer in print, however larger libraries should be able to access them. (For a full bibliography of books on hysteria see Mark S. Micale's *Approaching Hysteria: Disease and Its Interpretations*, an exhaustive listing of key texts on the subject from the early classical period to the present, with a helpfully critical gloss.) I have divided these notes into a section on psychology and literature, followed by a section on individual authors.

Psychology and Literature

Allen, Walter, *The English Novel: A Short Critical History* (Penguin, 1954)
For those who want to trace the 250- year history of the English novel - from *Pilgrim's Progress* to James Joyce and D.H. Lawrence - without enrolling on a course.

Beer, Gillian *Arguing with the Past: Essays in Narrative from Woolf to Sidney* (Routledge, 1989)
Innovative and compelling essays which pay equal attention to the context in which particular novels were written, as well as the reading process that stems from it.

Beizer, Janet, *Ventriloquized Bodies: Narratives of Hysteria in Nineteenth Century France* (Cornell, 1994)
Elaborates 'the hystericization of aesthetics and culture' during the last half of the nineteenth century, by way of the 'hystericized novel'. Janet Beizer begins with the surrealists Louis Aragon and Andre Breton and their Romantic predecessors who believed that hysteria was 'the greatest poetic discovery at the end of the nineteenth century', too important to be left to the physicians. Beizer suggests that this influence was two-way, as shown by the literary style of medical texts from the period. These ideas are explored through readings of texts by Flaubert, Louise Colet, the Goncourts, Zola, and Rachilde.

Bernheim, Hippolyte *Bernheim's New Studies in Hypnotism* translated by Richard S. Sandor (International Universities Press, 1980)
Surprisingly readable and contemporary in feel, these essays make it quickly

obvious that although the psychology pioneers who are remembered today are Charcot and Freud, Bernheim and Pierre Janet were clearly up there with them.

Bernheimer, Charles and Kahane, Claire, eds, *In Dora's Case: Freud - Hysteria - Feminism* (Virago, 1985)
The collection of essays that reheated the debate about Freud's (mistaken) views on feminine sexuality.

Brooks, Peter *Psychoanalysis and Storytelling* (Oxford University Press, 1992) *Reading for the Plot* (Harvard University Press, 1984)
In both these books Peter Brooks starts with the assumption that psychoanalytic literary criticism has made a bad name for itself, and that he hopes to except himself from this rule. He agrees with Freud that sexuality and narrative form share common elements, and that stories are vital to human existence. His aim, an admirable one, is to show that the connections between psychoanalysis and literature can be enriching, rather than reductive.

Cummings, Katherine *Telling Tales: The Hysteric's Seduction in Fiction and Theory* (Stanford University Press, 1991)
A deconstructive reading of three classic texts - *Clarissa, Bleak House,* and *Tender is the Night* - which takes as its focus Freud's theory of seduction.

David-Menard, Monique, *Hysteria from Freud to Lacan: Body and Language in Psychoanalysis* translated by Catherine Porter (Cornell University Press, 1989)
Ambitious project which redefines the relation of language and the body in terms of Freud's theories of hysteria and Lacan's theory of jouissance. Monique David-Menard demonstrates how the language of the hysterical body becomes readable when mapped on to linguistic structures. Not for the faint-theoretically-hearted.

Evans, Martha Noel *Fits and Starts: A Genealogy of Hysteria in Modern France* (Cornell University Press, 1991)
An intellectual and cultural history of hysteria in France from the ferment produced by Charcot to the end of the 1980s, when Lacanian ideas were riding high. Martha Noel Evans looks in particular at the clash between psychiatry and psychoanalysis, and discusses dozens of influential figures and over a hundred theoretical texts. Broad, general, with passing reference made to literature.

Forrester, John *Language and the Origins of Psychoanalysis* (Macmillan, 1980) Serious discussion of early psychoanalytic problems.

Freud, Ernst L., *Letters of Sigmund Freud* (Hogarth, 1961)
A general selection of Freud's letters, with inevitable gaps, which nonetheless gives insight into the leaps of thought that are often lost when Freud's papers are read in the Standard Edition (abbreviated to SE) of his works.

Freud, Sigmund, 'Project for a Scientific Psychology' (1950) SE1p.283
Written in the 1880s, when Freud was beginning his career in psychology, this paper tries to get the human mind to conform to a scientific model; ultimately Freud fails, but his efforts are impressive, if only because he has the audacity to tackle real problems of psychic functioning head on.

Freud, Sigmund & Breuer, Joseph, *Studies on Hysteria* (1895) SE2
On a first reading Freud and Breuer appear to agree on the important issues of hysteria. However differences in their thinking, and especially their attitudes to patients, soon surface. While these cases on individual female patients can, as Freud surmised, be read as short stories, they are curiously neglectful - necessarily so - of the characters surrounding the hysterical heroine.

Freud, Sigmund *The Interpretation of Dreams* (1905) SE 5
The book that many claim must be read for an understanding of Freud; perhaps so, but only when the reader feels willing, rather than dutiful. Moreover it is much too big to read in bed; less that it will make you dream, or be too heavy to hold, as that it may put you to sleep.

Fragment of an Analysis of a Case of Hysteria (1915) SE 7
Hardly a fragment, but a small opus, and one which has got the backs up of two generations of young women. Dora is the Joan of Arc of Freud criticism, a young woman who was, so it goes, set up by Freud to prove his dubious findings on female sexuality. Despite its unpopularity with feminists this book is rivetting, humanly compelling, and can be read - unlike much of Freud's writings - without having to chase surrounding references. Read it before making up your own mind on Freud's views of women, suspending your reactions until the end.

Three Essays on the Theory of Sexuality (1905) SE 7
Another contentious and surprisingly lengthy essay (that became a book) which keeps outrunning its aims. Long discussions of masturbation and penis envy, much of which contemporary psychotherapists prefer to keep in historical parenthesis.

'Hysterical Phantasies and their Relation to Bisexuality' (1908) SE 9, p.157
At the time, this paper was highly contentious: it proposed that women's hysterical phantasies were often about other women, something which seems less contentious, and less indignant, nowadays.

'On the Sexual Theories of Children' (1908) SE 9, p.207

Inspired by the Little Hans case, in which a little boy elaborates increasingly frightening fantasies about his parent's intercourse. In it Freud insists that our desire for knowledge extends from our childhood need to know all about sex, and hence can be inhibited by a child's never finding out what he or she needs to know.

' "Civilised" Sexual Morality and Modern Nervous Illness' (1908) SE 9, p.179

This paper is written with almost Tolstoyan conviction, fluency, and suppressed anger: society's ills stem from sexual dilemmas arising from the misinformation surrounding women's sexual education and the contradictions surrounding men's.

'Family Romances' (1909) SE 9, p.239

A short paper which highlights a distinction between the biological facts of human reproduction and the emotional wishes which bring them to life. These wishes make the stories surrounding one's own conception - based on the heroism of oneself and one's parents - as unlikely to others as they are compelling to the individual who believes them.

'On the Universal Tendency to Debasement in the Sphere of Love' (1912) SE 11, p.179

Similar in tone to ' "Civilised" Sexual Morality and Modern Nervous Illness', this is a heartfelt discussion of why it is a bad idea to over-idealise the loved object - because it leads to contempt for any future lover as well as loathing for oneself.

'Those Wrecked by Success' (1916) SE 14, p.316

Psychological literary criticism which relates directly to findings Freud made - in particular about the unconscious motivation behind women's need to suffer - in his metapsychology papers.

Gallop, Jane, *The Daughter's Seduction: Feminism and Psychoanalysis* (Cornell, 1982)

A heated feminist reading of Freud's notion of Oedipal desire, focusing on the father-daughter seduction, which highlights the degree to which a kind of seduction often lies behind our impulse to interpret novels - and the world.

Gilbert, Sandra and Gubar, Susan, *The Madwoman in the Attic: The Woman Writer and the Nineteenth Century Literary Imagination* (Yale University Press, 1979)

A feminist rereading of classic realist novels which starts from the assumption that 'woman' is a metaphor for the body of the text (pen = phallus), and objects - with vehemence - to the idea that creativity is an inherently masculine activity.

Gilman, Sander L.; King, Helen; Porter, Roy; Rousseau, G.S.; Showalter, Elaine, *Hysteria Beyond Freud* (University of California Press, 1993)
A collection of contemporary essays which embraces hysteria as an ancient disease, hysteria as a symptom of the early modern world, and hysteria as a modern - and infinitely interpretable - problem.

Gordon, Dillian, 'Helene Rouart in Her Father's Study', in *Degas: Images of Women* (Liverpool, Tate, 1992), pp.18-23
Large format illustrated essays focusing on Degas' perception of women.

Maxim Gorky, *Reminiscences of Tolstoy, Chekhov and Andreev*, translated by Katherine Mansfield, S.S. Koteliansky, and Leonard Woolf (Hogarth, 1934)
Thoughtful, witty, and occasionally profound reflections on three men who helped shape Russian literature, which while shedding new light yet leaves many of Gorky's questions unanswered.

Geahchan, Dominique J. 'Haine et Identification Negative dans l'Hysterie', *Revue Francaise Psychoanalyse*, 3-1973, pp.337-57
Probing analysis of a painful potential within many women's development, in which hate for the feminine becomes fixed when the woman - a daughter - identifies negatively with her mother.

Green, Andre *On Private Madness* (Hogarth, 1974)
A sensitive interpreter of Lacan as well as a probing thinker in his own right, this collection of essays demonstrates why Andre Green is a renowned French psychoanalyst. The essays are steeped in clinical material which throws new light on psychic life, at least for readers willing to follow his periodically dense prose.

Gunn, Daniel *Psychoanalysis and Fiction: An Exploration of Literary and Psychoanalytic Borders* (Cambridge University Press, 1988)
Investigates the ways in which psychoanalytic writing and some creative fiction have common concerns and methods. Daniel Gunn examines the writings of psychoanalysts from Freud to Lacan, including recent French analysts like Maud Mannoni and Serge Leclaire, together with creative writers like Proust, Kafka, Samuel Beckett, and Marguerite Duras. A Lacanian influence is evident, although not heavily.

Hazell, Stephen, ed. *The English Novel: Developments in Criticism Since Henry James* (Macmillan, 1978)
Collection of classic essays, including Henry James 'The Art of Fiction' 1884, D.H. Lawrence 'Morality and the Novel' 1925, Lionel Trilling 'Manners, Morals, and the Novel' 1948, Angus Wilson 'Trust the Tale' 1963.

Irigaray, Luce *Speculum of the Other Woman* translated by Gillian C. Gill (Cornell University Press, 1985)
Reclaims hysteria for feminists through the hysterical practice of mimicry, with the aim of undoing Freud's opposition between perversion and hysteria, as well as masculinity and femininity.

Janet, Pierre *Psychological Healing: A Historical and Clinical Study* translated by Eden and Cedar Paul (G. Allen & Unwin, 1925) 2 vols
The surprising thing about Janet's prolific writings - of which this book is one of many volumes - apart from his relative neglect alongside Charcot and Freud, is his willingness to take the reader into his clinical world.

Jones, Ernest *Sigmund Freud: Life and Work* (Hogarth, 1953) 2 vols.
Although this biography is now less widely read than other Freud biographies - such as Peter Gay's - these volumes provide a wealth of insight into its subject.

Kahane, Claire, *Passions of the Voice: Hysteria, Narrative, and the Figure of the Speaking Woman, 1850-1915* (John Hopkins University Press, 1995)
This book argues that the subversion of gender definitions promoted by feminism in the late nineteenth century had an unsettling effect on literature of the time. Claire Kahane concentrates on the figure of the speaking woman - and specifically the way the narrative voice loses control of the story it is telling. There are chapters on Freud's Dora, Alice James' Diary, Olive Schreiner's *The Story of an African Farm*, Henry James' *The Bostonians*, Virginia Woolf's *The Voyage Out*, Conrad's *The Heart of Darkness*, and Ford Madox Ford's *The Good Soldier*. Kahane draws attention to the effects of a 'discourse in crisis' and of the narrator's compensatory attempts to regain control of it. She concludes that for modernist writers hysteria was not a pathology but a sign of the times. But be warned, Kahane's text is psychoanalytic in an academically dense way and is apt to lose the unwary general reader.

Kofman, Sarah, *The Childhood of Art* translated by W. Woodhull (Columbia University Press, 1988)
A sophisticated reading of Freud's views on art and artists, which refuses to simplify the problems involved in thinking about how art comes into being.
The Enigma of Woman: Woman in Freud's Writings translated by Catherine Porter (Cornell University Press, 1985)
After discussing Freud's early attitudes to women, Sarah Kofman presents forceful yet subtle readings of 'On Narcissism', 'Femininity', and other works, to show that Freud's interest in women extended from fascination to fear. Links are made to ideas by Lacan, Derrida, and Irigaray.

Kristeva, Julia *Black Sun: Depression and Melancholia* translated by Leon S. Roudiez (Columbia University Press, 1989)
Takes the view that depression is a discourse with a language to be learned, rather than a pathology to be physically treated. Julia Kristeva makes an analogy between an ennui at the heart of Western civilization today and a pervasive loss of values - a black sun that could eclipse our social being as a whole.

Lacan, Jacques *The Four Fundamental Concepts of Psycho-Analysis* ed. by Jacques-Alain Miller, translated by Alan Sheridan (Penguin, 1979)
If psycho-analysis is a science, Lacan suggests, it may be similar to linguistics; hence the need to clarify the meaning of the four fundamental concepts: the drive, repetition, the unconscious, and transference. One of Lacan's more readable translated texts which explores his views on religion, alienation, sexuality, and death.

Laplanche, Jean *Life and Death in Psychoanalysis* translated by Jeffrey Mehlman (John Hopkins University Press, 1976)
Although Jean Laplanche is clearly influenced by Lacanian theory, this book shows his emergence from it. Unafraid of taking on Freud head-on, this is a fresh - but demanding - essay on the fundamentals of human life.

Laplanche, Jean & Pontalis, J.-B. *The Language of Psycho-Analysis* translated by Donald Nicholson-Smith (Hogarth, 1985)
A cross between a dictionary and an encyclopaedia with over 500 entries – in a readable style.

Lemoine-Luccioni, Eugenie *The Dividing of Women or Woman's Lot* translated by Marie-Laure Davenport and Marie-Christine Reguis (Free Association Books, 1987)
A study of the thoughts and fantasies of pregnant women in psychoanalysis which presents childbirth as a crisis of separation which women resolve differently. The clinical material is integrated with discussions of femininity, beauty, and spirituality in Western culture.

Jeffrey M. Masson, ed. *Complete Letters of Sigmund Freud to Wilhelm Fliess* (Harvard, 1992)
An excellent resource for readers willing to make their own minds up about Freud's theories on sexuality, as well as being a fascinating record of a friendship.

Micale, Mark, *Approaching Hysteria: Disease and Its Interpretation* (Princeton University Press, 1995)
A meticulous, scholarly A-Z of hysteria which mentions every key text from the early classical period to the present, with a critical gloss. Part One traces

hysteria as a medical disease, Part Two looks at hysteria as a cultural metaphor. This is a 'primary' secondary text that synthesises a vast range of material and organises it under conceptual headings; it is unrivalled in its intellectual command of the topic.

Herman Nunberg and Ernst Federn, *The Minutes of the Vienna Psychoanalytic Society* (International Universities Press, 1967), vol. 2
These volumes give an invaluable insight into, and summary of, the kinds of arguments and points of agreement that brought the earliest psychoanalysts together every Wednesday evening, when they met to discuss psychological topics.

Segal, Hanna 'The Achievement of Ambivalence' *Common Knowledge* Spring 1992, pp.92-103
Instead of suggesting that ambivalence (the presence of conflictual feelings) is something best overcome, Hanna Segal gives a convincing case for ambivalence as an achievement in itself.

Showalter, Elaine *The Female Malady: Women, Madness and English Culture* 1830-1980 (Virago, 1987)
This book shows how cultural ideas about 'proper' feminine behaviour have shaped the definition and treatment of female insanity for 150 years, as well as giving mental disorders in women a sexual meaning. Elaine Showalter describes key psychiatrists, drawing on the diaries and narratives of their patients, alongside fiction from Mary Wollstonecraft to Doris Lessing, to provide a cultural perspective on the study of mental illness. This remains a well-known 'hysteria book'; it is broadly social history, with reference to literature, theatre, and art. The historical span is wide, the selection of secondary documentation fascinating, and the conclusions fairly open.

Smith, Joseph H. 'Primitive Guilt' in *Pragmatism's Freud: The Moral Disposition of Psychoanalysis* (Johns Hopkins University, 1986)
A straightforward account of a concept which is as hard to explain as it is painful to bear.

Sully, James *Sensation and Intuition: Studies in Psychology and Aesthetics* (Henry King, 1874)
Readable and rich account of early psychological insights.

Winnicott, D.W. *Family and Individual Development* (Tavistock, 1965)
The account of spoiling in this volume gives a generous and nuanced view of what is perhaps an inevitable moment in every individual's development.

Individual Authors

Balzac

Balzac, Honore de, *La Comedie humaine*, 12 vols, ed. by Pierre-Georges Castex, and others; a revision of the 1935 Pleiade edition (Gallimard, 1976-1981)

'Avant-propos', Pleiade, vol. 1, p.7

In this essay Balzac declares his intentions - to describe human nature as it is, rather than as many of us would have it be. The trouble is that Balzac wrote it before his project assumed the vast dimensions that it finally did.

Eugenie Grandet (Gallimard, Collection Folio, 1979]

Eugenie Grandet translated by Sylvia Raphael (OUP World's Classics, 1990)

La Femme de Trente Ans, Pleiade, vol. 8

Balzac makes his first plea on behalf of the mature woman, showing her superiority over insipid younger women in her depths of passion, and extends her love life beyond the conventional age-limit.

Le Lys de la vallée, Pleiade, vol. 9, p.969

This story, written close in time to *Eugenie Grandet*, is a young man's account of his affair with the young wife of a hypochondriachal, middle-aged husband. It begins with the young man's adoration of the woman's shoulders at a ball. An unlikely but fascinating study of an emotional triangle - plus the woman's two children.

Physiologie du mariage Pleiade, vol. 11, p.193

Written around the time of *Eugenie Grandet*, in an enquiring style which is no longer fashionable - hence the absence of English translations. It is the story of a young couple's apprehensions and misapprehensions of marriage, told through the eyes of an ironic narrator. It is a light-hearted, witty guide for the husband-to-be which gives the warning signs of his wife's (inevitable) infidelity, in a style which is sensitive without being coarse. Crystallises marital crises which afflict the unprepared with - for the time - an unusual sympathy for the frustrations of women that are so often their trigger. Works better as a series of related scenes than as an organic novel.

'The Red Inn' *Balzac: Selected Short Stories* translated by Sylvia Raphael (Penguin, 1977)

Faultlessly told story about human greed and the power of a dead man's money to fascinate yet repel his daughter's suitor.

Bertault, Philippe *Balzac and the Human Comedy* (New York University Press, 1963)

Intelligent account of Balzac's project, including a biographical sketch, and detailed analyses of the characters, stories, and techniques within it.

Brooks, Peter *The Melodramatic Imagination* (Yale University press, 1986)
According to Brooks' interpretation of melodrama, the reader gets a thrill out
of stories like Eugenie's because he or she secretly identifies with the fickle
Charles and the gloating Grandet - that is, the reader can't help but dread
yet delight in the heroine's fate.

Hunt, *Comedie Humaine* (Athlone Press, University of London, 1959)
Descriptive history of the *Comedie Humaine* (1829-1848) which puts the
novels and stories into chronological and thematic order.

Kanes, Martin, ed. *Critical Essays on Honore de Balzac* (G.K. Hall, 1990)
Balzac may have set out to describe the world, to be the 'secretary of society',
but as Kane points out (in his essay in this collection) Balzac's ultimate role
was as interpreter - creator - of his society.

Prendergast, Christopher *Balzac: Fiction and Melodrama* (Edward Arnold,
1978)
The aim of melodrama, in its traditional form, is to present an uncomplicated
moral picture of the world which frees the individual from doubt,
uncertainty, and ambiguity. But it has a further more subtle aim, which is
to invite the reader into an imaginative world that allows him or her to shift
between a longing for order and a fascination with disorder.

Charlotte Brontë

Allott, Miriam *The Brontës: The Critical Heritage* (Routledge, Kegan & Paul,
1974)
Comprehensive volume which presents chronologically initial reactions to
Villette, followed by more recent, and equally contentious, criticism of the
novel.

Brontë, Charlotte *The Poems of Charlotte Brontë* ed. by Tom Winnifrith
(Blackwell, 1984)
These poems, beautifully edited, give fascinating insight into the shaping
forces behind Charlotte Brontë's creativity.
Villette ed. by Mark Lilly (Penguin, 1981)
The Spell: An Extravaganza ed. by George E. Maclean (Oxford University
Press, 1936)
Worth reading, if only to realise how far Charlotte Brontë had come in her
mastery of the novel by the time of writing *Villette*.

Dooley, Laura 'The Psychoanalysis of C. Brontë, as a Type of the Woman of
Genius', *American Journal of Psychology* 31, July 1920, pp.221-72
Psychoanalytic criticism as it used to be: bold, diagnostic, and unashamably
Oedipal in its interpretations.

Gaskell, Elizabeth *The Life of Charlotte Brontë* (Penguin, 1985)
Admirably honest and informal biography, given the conventions of biography of the period, as well as Gaskell's neighbourly relations with the Brontë family.

Guerin, Winifred *The Brontës* (Longman, 1973)
Reliable biographical account divided into four parts; gives a vivid sense of Charlotte Brontë in the midst of family and friends.

Maynard, Roger *Charlotte Brontë and Sexuality* (Cambridge University Press, 1984)
A brave but ultimately brazen interpretation of Charlotte Brontë's literary project as motivated by suppressed passions.

Ratchford, Fanny E. *The Brontë's Web of Childhood* (Columbia University Press, 1941)
Fascinating journey into a childhood that few children will again enjoy; a childhood in which stories appear more real than life itself, with life coming second to imagination.

Wise, Thomas J. and Symington, John A. eds. *The Brontës: Their Lives, Friendships and Correspondences in Four Volumes* (Oxford Head, 1933)
These volumes are as impossible to read right through as they are to put down wherever they are picked up; together they successfully undermine any attempt to characterise Charlotte Brontë in a schematic way.

Tolstoy

Berlin, Isiah *The Hedgehog and the Fox: An Essay on Tolstoy's View of History* (Weidenfeld, 1988)
The fox knows many things, but the hedgehog knows just one big thing. In this study Berlin supposes that Tolstoy was by nature a fox but by preference a hedgehog.

Kisseleff, Natasha 'Idyll and Ideal: Aspects of Sentimentalism in Tolstoy's "Family Happiness"' *Modern Critical Views: Leo Tolstoy* ed. by Harold Bloom (Chelsea House, 1986), pp.211-20
A thoughtful essay which seeks to explain why Tolstoy rejected a sentimentalist approach to literature following the publication of 'Family Happiness'.

Maude, Aylmer *The Life of Tolstoy* (Oxford University Press, 1987 (1908))
If you want to read a life of Tolstoy it may be this one; interest and time permitting you might read Henri Troyat's life alongside it, since only then will you realise how selective even the longest biography inevitably is.

Family Views of Tolstoy (G. Allen & Unwin, 1926)
A collection of essays which, read together, builds up an anecdotal and insightful picture of Tolstoy the man.

Poggioli, Renato 'Tolstoy's "Domestic Happiness"', *Tolstoy's Short Fiction*, ed. by M. Katz (Norton, 1991)
Suggests that in both *War and Peace* and 'Domestic Happiness' it is 'the self-same institution, the family, that triumphs over the powers of disorder, over the chaos of either passion or war'. But 'unlike *War and Peace*, 'Domestic Happiness' is a fable with a moral. The moral is that life chastises those who think that life is a dream. It is a sign of Tolstoy's artistic stature that despite the personal motivations that dictated the writing of this story, he chose to have Masha chastened by life rather than by her husband, in whom he portrayed himself' (p.411).

Tolstoy, Leo *Childhood, Boyhood, Youth* translated by Rosemary Edmonds (Penguin, 1965)
The Death of Ivan Ilyich and Other Stories (includes 'Family Happiness' as 'Happiness Ever After') translated by Rosemary Edmonds (Penguin, 1964)
Tolstoy's Letters translated by R.F. Christian, 2 vols 1828-79 (Athlone, 1978)
Although Tolstoy was no 'letter-writer's letter writer' he wrote a prolific number of letters – 32 of his 90 – volume Soviet edition are taken up by over 8500 of them. This extensive collection is oddly compelling, perhaps because it identifies three Tolstoys: Tolstoy the writer (his views of his own work and that of other writers), Tolstoy the thinker (his attitudes to society, rural life, education, and spirituality), and Tolstoy the man (his relation to family and friends, and the development of his personality). Even a skim through this collection is a helpful counter to the selective extracts from Tolstoy's letters quoted in biographies.
Tolstoy's Diaries translated by R.F. Christian, 2 vols (Athlone)
Spanning 63 years, from 1847 when Tolstoy began at Kazan University, to November 1920 as he lay dying at a provincial railway station, these entries chart, in an intimate way, his artistic and spiritual career. During his youth he wrote with a candidness that assumes no audience but himself (his first entry is written from a venereal disease clinic). His aims in the diary are less literary than psychological: to monitor his relations with himself and others, to cultivate his faculties, and to define his future - and the fact that he often fails these aims makes the diary more not less interesting.

Wasiolek, Edward *Tolstoy's Major Fiction* (University of Chicago, 1978)
Readable commentaries on the larger works which sets Tolstoy in a cultural context, while highlighting the specificity of his approach to literature - his

questing spirit, his insistence on realism, and his search for a balance between individual and social moralities.

George Eliot

Eliot, George *Daniel Deronda* ed. by Barbara Hardy (Penguin, 1976)
Daniel Deronda ed. by George Handley (Clarendon Press, 1984)
Complete edition with fascinating annotations from the manuscript.
The Essays of George Eliot ed. by George Pinney (Routledge, Kegan & Paul, 1963)
Selected Critical Writings of George Eliot ed. by Rosemary Ashton (OUP World's Classics, 1992)

Haight, Gordon S. *George Eliot: A Biography* (Oxford University Press, 1986)
A classic biography which rewards reading.

Korg, Jacob, 'How George Eliot's People Think', *George Eliot: A Centenary Tribute* ed. by Gordon S. Haight & Rosemary VanArsdel (Macmillian, 1982)
Makes the point that although George Eliot maintained that the mind is inherently regulated and subject to cause and effect, that her actual characters – especially her heroines – are anything but regulated inside their minds. When characters who are otherwise autonomous lose control of themselves, and 'drop the reins of their fate' the reader feels – with them –that 'quality of bewilderment' that characterises George Eliot's later novels.

Sadoff, Dianne *Monsters of Affection: Dickens, Eliot and Brontë on Fatherhood* (John Hopkins University Press, 1982)
An unabashedly psychoanalytic study of three women writers which assumes that each was subject to a Victorian ambivalence to paternal authority - 'the desire for its stability, decisiveness, and cultural validity side by side with the hatred of its narrowness, stubbornness, and social domination of those without such authority' (p.6).

Uglow, Jennifer *George Eliot* (Virago, 1987)
Provocative appraisal of George Eliot and her work which looks at the author's conflictual attitudes to Victorian life and the position of women within it, as enlivened by a powerful imaginative drive.

Yeazell, Ruth Bernard, ed. *Sex, Politics and Science in the Nineteenth Century Novel* (John Hopkins University Press, 1986)
This collection includes essays by Gillian Beer, 'Origins and Oblivion in Victorian Narrative', and Catherine Gallagher, 'George Eliot and *Daniel Deronda*'.

Florence Nightingale

Allen, Donald R. 'Florence Nightingale: Toward a Psychohistorical Interpretation', *Journal of Interdisciplinary History* Summer 1975, no. 6, pp.23-54
Slightly heavy-handed analysis of Florence Nightingale's motivations.

Cook, Sir Edward *The Life of Florence Nightingale* (Macmillan, 1914), 2 vols.
Standard biographical account which concentrates on Florence Nightingale's public life and profile.

O'Malley, Ida Beatrice *Florence Nightingale 1820-1856: A Study of her Life Down to the End of the Crimean War* (Thornton Butterworth)
Uncritical account of the younger Florence Nightingale with helpful inclusion of hard-to-come-by diary and letter extracts.

Nightingale, Florence *Notes from the Devotional Authors of the Middle Ages, collected, chosen and freely translated by Florence Nightingale (1872-93)* (British Library Manuscripts, Add. 45841
The title itself reflects the sincerity and looseness of this collection of inspired writings.
Notes on Nursing: What it is, and What it is not (Gerald Duckworth, 1852)
A no-nonsense handbook on current nursing practice and recommended reforms of it.
Suggestions for Thought and Cassandra ed. by Mary Poovey (Chatto and Pickering, 1991)
Intriguing but finally frustrating edition, primarily because the really interesting parts of 'Cassandra' are only available in manuscript; with the result that despite meticulous editing the work as a whole fails to cohere.
Suggestions for Thought (Eyre and Spottiswoode, 1860) 2 vols.
A privately published edition, distributed to selected friends and acquaintances.
Suggestions for Thought British Library Manuscripts, Add. 45839
The original and fiercely corrected and edited version from which later editions were collated.

Showalter, Elaine 'Florence Nightingale's Feminist Complaint: Women, Religion and *Suggestions for Thought*', *Signs*, Spring 1981, pp.395-414
The article that set off my interest in Florence Nightingale's writings , leading to a subsequent meeting with Elaine Showalter, and her encouragement to read the original manuscripts in the British Library.

Strachey, Rachel *The Cause: A Short History of the Women's Movement* (Virago, 1978)

A reissue of a classic historical text which creates a sense of the turmoil surrounding women's liberation in the late nineteenth century.

Vicinus, Martha and Nergaard, Bea, eds. *Ever Yours, Florence Nightingale: Selected Letters* (Virago, 1989)
A vast resource as well as a fascinating read.

Index